THOUGH I WALK
through the
VALLEY

STORIES OF TEARS, TRAUMA, AND TRIUMPH
DURING THE DARK DAYS OF DIVORCE

TIMOTHY W. SCOTT

Copyright © 2022 Timothy W. Scott
All rights reserved
First Edition

Fulton Books
Meadville, PA

Published by Fulton Books 2022

ISBN 979-8-88505-609-0 (paperback)
ISBN 979-8-88505-610-6 (digital)

Printed in the United States of America

This book is dedicated to all my friends and family who walked beside me as I walked through the valley. Most of all to my parents, Delbert and Donna, who were there every step of the way.

Contents

Foreword vii
Acknowledgment ix
Preface..xi
Introduction xv

Section 1: The Conflict 1

Chapter 1:   Rejection 3
Chapter 2:   Dark Days..13
Chapter 3:   Emotional Exhaustion 19
Chapter 4:   Shame 27
Chapter 5:   Triggers 33

Section 2: The Cry for Help...39

Chapter 6:   Loneliness 41
Chapter 7:   Should I Have Done More 49
Chapter 8:   Worse than Death 56

Section 3: The Church 69

Chapter 9:   How Did I Become a Statistic? 71
Chapter 10: How Will the Church View Me? 75
Chapter 11: Help or Hinder? 82

Section 4: The Children of Divorce 89

Chapter 12: The Children of Divorce 91
Chapter 13: Save the Children 97
Chapter 14: Redemption 101

Section 5: Cultivating Healing 107

Chapter 15: Hope..109
Chapter 16: The Importance of Healing.....................................117
Chapter 17: Help in Healing (Friends and Family) 124
Chapter 18: Our Living Hope 130

Section 6: Coming Alive...139

Chapter 19: Loving Yourself...141
Chapter 20: Loving Others 145
Chapter 21: Loving God..152
Chapter 22: Living Life...158

Section 7: Carrying on with Confidence 163

Chapter 23: The Return of the King.......................................165

Conclusion...173
Appendix A: Advice for Someone Contemplating Divorce 177
Appendix B: Where Are They Now?......................................181
Appendix C: Scriptures and Translations Used 184

FOREWORD

In a world of sound bites and picture-perfect photo ops, the pain of divorce—especially in the church—can often be ignored. We see the polished veneer of people and rarely get to the heart of that one dealing with the less than perfect life. With *Though I Walk through the Valley*, Tim weaves his own experience along with that of others of both genders and different age groups with strong biblical reference and relevance, creating an undeniable picture of the human condition. You will hear his story and learn about who he is: where he came from, what values he was raised on, and what he and others interviewed have learned from the struggles of divorce and how they found hope through that pain.

I've known Tim and his family for many years. His life has always and foremost been about loving God and loving others. His life seemed to follow a predictable path and then came an unpredictable curve in the road—an unwanted divorce and the devastation a divorce brings. Emotions that vacillate from anger to guilt to despair. The situation made worse by social isolation—feelings of shame—initially too overwhelmed to let others know what he was going through.

Because a divorce is so complicated, Tim soon recognized that he was not alone in needing support. He had been taught that marriage was final and that God hates divorce, but he would also discover that God will love you through an unwanted divorce and embrace you in the midst of the pain and confusion. The lie that God helps only a picture-perfect family is just that…a lie. God's blessing is not just for intact families but for all who remain faithful to Him.

Though I Walk through the Valley is less like a book and more like a kitchen table conversation with a guy who is passionately committed to sharing his pain while offering encouragement to those who have and will walk this journey. *As a minister for more than fifty years, this book would've been a must-read for every couple I counseled that was experiencing the pain of divorce.* In reading this book, God will stretch your thinking and sensitize your heart to the heart of this painful reality.

A must-read for anyone interested in representing the real Jesus to a broken world.

Tim has chosen to not allow divorce to be the entire story of his life—choosing instead to believe that "God does work for the good of those who love Him, who have been called according to His purpose" (Romans 8:28). The reader will be encouraged by not only his story but those he chose to interview on this topic—those who all have been inspired to move forward.

Pastor Ernest G. Mullins

Acknowledgment

No big idea, project, or plan comes to fruition without the contribution of many people. When I sat out to write this book, I knew it would only be successful if I were able to share the stories of others who have walked through the difficult valley of divorce. In order to share their stories, though, I was asking them to be vulnerable without anything in return. Thank you to Alissa, Beth, Don, Tami, Susan, and Mark who agreed to be interviewed in hopes that their stories would help others.

Thank you to the others who allowed their stories to be told as well. To Kelly and Terry, your contributions to Chapter 8, "Worse than Death," are extremely valuable. To Jon, Shelby, Derek, Sheena, Rachel, and Amber, your willingness to share has given a voice to all the "children of divorce" who have felt the pain that you felt.

To my four editors—Corrie, Faith, Chrissy, and Gordon—you have made the book worth reading. Your hours of reading and correcting all my mistakes are an invaluable contribution to the book. I am forever indebted to each of you for your work.

To my support team and prayer warriors who have encouraged me and prayed for me during the writing of this book, I am deeply grateful. I have felt your prayers and believe that God has truly inspired during this process. Your behind-the-scenes support will have a lasting and positive effect on all those who read this written word.

Through the combined effort of all those mentioned above, this book became possible. It is my hope that it will be used by God as a tool to bring healing to all who read it.

Sincerely,
Tim

PREFACE

A friend once said to me, "You don't get a divorce; you go through a divorce." This statement is absolutely correct. Thinking someone can walk away from a marriage without consequence is one of the biggest lies of the devil. The trail of destruction left in the wake of a separation and eventual divorce is devastating. Like shock waves during an earthquake, this devastation expands to untold hundreds—if not thousands—of friends, family, and most of all, children of divorce. Divorce can be the most life-shattering event a child or a spouse will ever experience.

I know the trauma, feelings, and emotions. I've walked through the valley of divorce. However, I also know the peace and joy of Jesus coming alongside and walking with me. Today, 40 percent[1] of all marriages end in divorce. Therefore, a lot of people are walking this same lonely path. For someone who has never experienced it, understanding will be hard; but for someone standing at the beginning of the valley, the road ahead looks almost unbearable. Questions like "How do I face tomorrow?" "Does anyone understand what I am going through?" and "Will this ever end?" plague the mind of a spouse whose life they once knew now lays in a pile of broken hopes and dreams in front of them.

With this in mind, I began to reflect and wonder, *How could I help others who are beginning one of life's most difficult journeys?*

I decided it was time to write a book. However, this book would not just tell my journey; it would also tell the stories of several people who can now look back on the worst parts of their journey and give others perspective and hope. I began putting together a list of people I knew would be a good fit for this project.

I targeted a specific demographic. Obviously, those I chose were divorced, but they all had one other thing in common: each one grew

---

[1] https://divorcestrategiesgroup.com/why-second-marriages-fail

up in a stable Christian home. They all had parents who loved each other and loved them, and divorce was not a part of their heritage. Why was this important? Because there is an extra stigma attached or perceived if a person comes from a stable home and their family falls apart. I know; I am in this demographic.

I didn't know what response I would get when I contacted the people on my target list. Much to my surprise, each person on my list agreed to let me interview them as they told their stories. Many of them responded with "I'm happy to tell my story if it will help others" (or something similar.)

As I began the interview process, something else amazing happened. In every case, at some point before, during, or after the interview, each of them began asking me questions about *my* story. Since they had all gone through a divorce, their hearts went out to me, as I was not as far along the path as they were. Through their experiences, they hurt for those who hurt.

Some of their stories began much differently. Some were abandoned by their spouse and experienced the pain of an unfaithful partner. A handful had experienced verbal and even physical abuse while others readily admitted their divorce was caused by their own unfaithfulness or unwise decision. It didn't matter why it began; all of them had been forced to walk the difficult path of divorce.

This book does not tell the stories of what caused the divorce. You won't find the names of or the stories about ex-spouses in this book. If you are looking for a guide to save your marriage, you have come to the wrong place. If you want a book about why you should or shouldn't divorce or remarry again, you will be disappointed.

This book is directed at three specific groups of people:

1. If you are contemplating a divorce, this book is for you. Do not believe Satan's lies of walking away will be easy; it simply is not true. You will experience quite possibly the darkest days of your life, and it is a difficult journey.
2. If you are beginning or are in the valley of divorce, this book is written for you. Sometimes divorce is inevitable. Other times, you are forced to travel this difficult path,

even though you didn't choose to. If this is you, the stories in this book will change your outlook on life and, if you let it, will truly change your life. You are not alone.
3. If you know someone who is divorced, separated, or contemplating divorce, this book is a must-read for you. This group of people is not very specific; most everyone will fit into this category. So why should you read this? You should read it to understand better and hopefully help those you know who are going through this traumatic period in their lives. Once you know the pain, observe the hurt, discern the internal thoughts, and experience the stories of this ever-growing segment of society, you will begin to truly understand how your kind words and actions are capable of dramatically helping to heal a broken heart. You can change a life.

One more thing. If you believe God is a fairy tale or that He simply looks down on the world but is not a personal god, this book will significantly challenge that belief. I did not commence with intentions of writing a book about the faithfulness of God, but the stories I heard make it impossible to tell about the journey without including the one who came to give us life "more abundantly."[2] The most incredible healing takes place when you know and allow the "Great Physician" to work in your life.

Now, it's time to come along with me as we experience the journeys of seven people who have walked one of life's most difficult paths. Their stories will make you smile, make you cry, make you hurt, and make you care. Through it all, you will be inspired by these accounts, and your eyes will be opened to the hurting people all around you.

Please note: While their stories are real, some names have been changed in order to provide moderate anonymity to those interviewed. However, they agreed to let their story be written in order to give hope to others who have had to walk a similar path.

---

[2] John 10:10 (KJV)

INTRODUCTION

As young David peered down at the Kidron Valley, he could feel his heartbeat increase. He wished there was some way that he could avoid going through this valley. It wasn't a long journey by foot from Bethlehem to Jerusalem; in fact, David could see Jerusalem just beyond the valley. However, this final and most treacherous part of his journey was filled with unlimited fear and danger.

For David to reach the valley, he first had to face a steep and dangerous path that was also very narrow and rugged. Each step had to be made with caution, or it could be his last. However, he couldn't just look at his feet as there were lions and bears in the area that could attack and easily kill an unsuspecting traveler. David was well aware of this, as he had killed both lions and bears just a few miles away as he tended his father's sheep. However, he also knew the lion or the bear could easily be the victor the next time. Yes, this valley brought fear into the heart of anyone who dared to enter.

Once in the valley, the danger continued. The valley was so steep and deep at specific points that the sun only overtook the shadows when it was directly overhead. The rest of the time, the shadows produced a cover for thieves waiting to attack a weary traveler and to steal any possessions by any means necessary. Many travelers had been beaten and robbed in this valley.

If David made it through these pitfalls, he would have to walk through a massive burial ground. As he neared his destination, the trail was lined with graves and caves. The idea of a burial ground would scare any traveler no matter their age, and it was enough to paralyze a young boy with fear. These fears may be why David would later refer to the Kidron Valley in Psalm 23 by its other name, "the valley of the shadow of death."

One of the deepest valleys anyone will ever have to walk is the valley of divorce. When you stand at the rim of this valley and look at the road ahead, the darkness and despair can seem almost insurmountable. Like the Kidron Valley, divorce can seem like the valley of the shadow of death. As you begin to descend into the valley, the road looks scary, and each step seems to take you deeper and deeper into the unknown.

Times will come when you will feel the oppression of your great enemy, Satan, as "he prowls around like a roaring lion,"[3] seeking to devour you. Fear, doubt, anger, and bitterness are some of his greatest weapons. You cannot look down, as you must remain vigilant and ever watchful of his attacks.

There will be many days when it seems like the sun will never shine again. At that moment, a glimmer of sunlight may appear for a few brief moments before you, once again, find yourself back in the shadows. As you walk through the valley, questions come with each interaction. Is this person my friend or a foe? Are they here to help, or are they enemies waiting to attack and rob me of any bit of security and dignity I have left? What do they really think about me? Who can I trust, and who do I need to avoid?

Quite possibly, the most challenging part of the valley to traverse is the graveyard. Look closely, and you will see the graves of broken promises, shattered dreams, betrayal, rejection, loneliness, and lost hope, to name a few. Each grave represents something you have lost. Make no mistake; there is plenty that will be lost.

However, with each step, obstacles will begin to fade into the distance, and the sun will start to shine again. The more extended amounts of sunshine feel great, but when you are starting your journey through the valley, the promise of reprieve sounds like a very distant dream. What you want to know is, "How am I supposed to navigate the valley of the shadow of death that lies ahead?"

Come with me and hear the stories of others who have walked through this dark valley of divorce and have emerged on the other side. While every story is different, each has some common threads. Every person interviewed grew up in a stable Christian home with parents who loved them and loved each other. However, each of them would find themselves walking through the valley of divorce.

---

[3] 1 Peter 5:8 (NLT)

Some of you, like Mark, know you are on this journey because of your own poor decisions. Mark recalls that "seeing the disappointment in the faces of my family, my children, and my church friends was very, very difficult for me. Having to open up and let them know that I had failed in my marriage—I think that was the deepest and hardest part."

Maybe you are traveling this lonely path because you were abandoned by your spouse. Don knows this feeling. "It's the loss of a legacy," says Don. "The realization that the person I thought I knew wasn't who I thought she was. The loss of the years, the loss of trust, the loss of a relationship, the loss of something you really thought was there, wasn't there. The feeling of being betrayed was powerful, and the emotional and relational betrayal was palpable."

Susan knows the same rejection. "I didn't know what was true. I didn't know what was false because that had been so corrupted." She explained, "I didn't know, of those twenty-six years, if any of the love was true. What you think you know was turned around. It's a great betrayal of not knowing what part of your life is according to your memory or not. It's sad. I'll never have closure for that."

Maybe your story is similar to Alissa's. She lived in an abusive marriage for years but refused to let go. She was a fixer and was willing to do whatever it took to make her marriage work. Even though her family pleaded with her to get out, she continued to try. The day came, however, when she knew God was releasing her from the marriage. After years of enduring extreme abuse and rejection, she finally reached the point where she did what was best for her young child. "I would have sacrificed myself to the end," Alissa said, "but when you have a child, no longer is it just about you. I could no longer allow that for her." Even though Alissa did what she knew she had to do, she still struggled with her decision. Alissa recalled how hard it was to give it up. "It's hard to let go of a dream, even if the dream isn't a healthy one. The hardest part was surrendering what I thought it would be and what I wanted it to be."

Today, many people are walking through the valley of divorce for a second time. Statistics tell us that while 40 percent[4] of first marriages

---

[4] https://divorcestrategiesgroup.com/why-second-marriages-fail

end in divorce; the statistic jumps to a staggering 67 percent[5] of second marriages. Tami knows the struggles of multiple failed marriages. While she regrets the decision she made as a young mother to walk away from a struggling marriage, Tami knows full well the difficulty of seeing another spouse walk away from her. Today she says, "The biggest struggle for me was being a single parent. It wasn't easy. I had to rely on so many people. I don't like asking people for help, and I had no choice but to do so. Being a single parent was hard, and financially, it was very difficult."

Regardless of the reason for the divorce, we can all relate to Beth when she explains how the divorce left her "feeling like a failure and a fool. My dream of an ideal family was shot," she says. "I was by myself. I had nobody." Her dreams of having "two or three kids, buying a house with a little bit of acreage, hosting family get-togethers, having a big yard, and building a future" were now gone. For many years, Beth struggled with questions: Will I ever find love again? Is it even right for me to look for somebody who would love me? Beth also wondered if "I would ever find anyone that I felt was good enough for me that would accept me for now having those flaws."

If you are walking or have walked through the valley of divorce, you can relate to many of the stories, regrets, and feelings mentioned above. You can also empathize with King David in the Bible. His story doesn't involve divorce, but it very much consists in walking through many valleys. In fact, one of the most familiar scripture passages in the Bible, Psalm 23, was written as David was in a deep valley. He called it "the valley of the shadow of death." We will explore this story and Psalm 23 much deeper as we progress through the book.

While every story mentioned is filled with pain and sorrow, they are also filled with hope and healing. Each person's journey is filled with God's goodness, peace, and continued guidance. Notice the title, "though I walk THROUGH the valley." Each of those spoken of above has walked THROUGH the valley but has come out on the other side. You can do the same. My prayer is, as you read about others' journeys, you, too, will find help and hope for your own journey. Come along. It's time to walk "THROUGH" the valley together.

---

[5] https://divorcestrategiesgroup.com/why-second-marriages-fail

SECTION 1

The Conflict

> When you get to the point where you are facing divorce, it doesn't matter how you got there, you're there, and the end result is the same.
>
> —Mark

> *Since they are no longer two but one, let no one split apart what God had joined together.*
>
> *—Matthew 19:6 NLT*

MINISTER: Repeat after me:

> I, _____, take thee, _____, to be my lawfully wedded husband/wife.
> To have and to hold from this day forward.
> For better or for worse,
> For richer or for poorer,
> In sickness and in health,
> To love and to cherish,
> Till death do us part,
> According to God's holy ordinance;
> And thereto I pledge thee my faith.

MINISTER: I now pronounce you man and wife. What God has joined together, let no man put asunder. You may kiss the bride.

The cameras flash, the crowd claps, the minister introduces the new couple, the music begins to play, the couple walks down the aisle together, and the marriage officially begins. At that moment, the future looks like a never-ending story of happiness and bliss. You are married to the knight in shining armor or the beautiful princess you dreamed of for your whole life. Can this really be happening? Is this really true? Could your life really be turning out this well?

Hopefully, the answer to all these questions is a resounding "yes." Today may be the best first day of the rest of your life with many other wonderful days to follow. For many, however, the reality of binding yourself before God and man to another person is going to bring some of the greatest heartbreak humanity can ever experience. You do not really know that person standing beside you. In the years that follow, you will truly discover who they really are. You will also find out who you really are as well. God has joined you together; now it is up to the two of you to become one. How committed will you be to your wedding vows when the wedding bells become a distant memory? What happens when the vow of "I do" turns into a decision of "I don't"? That is the conflict, and what follows can turn any dream into a nightmare.

Rejection

> Of course I felt monumental rejection from the fact that my husband left and chose someone else.
>
> —Tami

> The world is made for married people. When you are single, you feel that rejection when they have a marriage seminar at church or a Valentine banquet or something. You feel that you are no longer part of that.
>
> —Susan

> *For God has said, "I will never fail you. I will never abandon you."*
>
> —*Hebrews 3:5b NLT*

Don's story

It was a beautiful June afternoon. It had been a while since Don had seen his parents, and Father's Day was just three days away. Don decided it was time to make the four-hour drive north to spend the weekend with them and celebrate Father's Day with his dad. Don's wife had to work that weekend but gave her blessing for him to make the trip alone. Don planned to spend this weekend with his parents, and the following weekend, he would spend with his wife as they celebrated their thirtieth wedding anniversary.

After Don got off work that Thursday night, he and his wife went out to eat before he left town for his three-day weekend. They finished eating, kissed goodbye, and went their separate ways. Little did he know that that kiss would be his last. Don went back by the house to finish packing. While there, he received a call from a family member telling him that his wife planned to move out that weekend while he was gone. He contacted her and received confirmation that it was true. She was done, she had moved on, and the marriage was over. The "I do" had become "I changed my mind."

Family rejection

The hurt caused by rejection is one of the greatest emotional pains a human can feel. That hurt is directly proportional to the closeness of the person who rejects you. When you are rejected by a distant friend, casual acquaintance, or maybe a stranger on the street, you will feel hurt or slighted; but the pain will be somewhat minimal. If that rejection comes from your inner circle of friends, the pain increases exponentially.

That rejection becomes much greater when it is carried out by a family member. A sibling, parent, or child possesses a great ability to destroy others in their immediate family emotionally. The same harsh words or actions enacted with very little effect by a stranger on the street can crush us when spoken or committed by a close family member. Why? Because of a little word called "love" and a big word called "vulnerability."

Your family knows you better than anyone else on earth. Most likely, you grew up in the same house, had many of the same experiences, laughed at the same jokes, and lived in the same environment. You grew to love your family not because you were supposed to, but because you couldn't help but love them. Before you were old enough to make a conscious decision to love, you were becoming bonded to them. After all, they were your "family."

As an infant, you began to "trust" those in your immediate family, becoming "vulnerable" to them without even realizing it. As you grew older, your family saw you on your worst days and most likely, you even fought occasionally, but despite the fights, in the end, you still knew the love never wavered. Your family knew your worst flaws, deepest faults, and darkest mistakes, yet they still loved you. Without even realizing it, you opened yourself up and gave them the weapons necessary to bring you to your knees; but you didn't worry about it because they were "family," and you could always trust your "family."

For some, you may have already experienced tremendous rejection from your family. It may be a parent that left you when you were young, or possibly you were abused growing up. You may know the hurt of a child turning their back on you and walking away. You may not feel, or have ever felt, the "love" of which I speak, but the hurt from being vulnerable and getting rejected is all too real.

Absalom's rejection of David

King David experienced this kind of love and rejection in the Bible. In 2 Samuel 15 (NLT), we find the story of King David and his son, Absalom. Beginning in verse 2, we read:

> He (Absalom) got up early every morning and went out to the gate of the city. When people brought a case to the king for judgment, Absalom would ask where in Israel they were from, and they would tell him their tribe.
> Then Absalom would say, "You've really got a strong case here! It's too bad the king doesn't have anyone to hear it. I wish I were the judge. Then everyone could bring their cases to me for judgment, and I would give them justice!"
> When people tried to bow before him, Absalom wouldn't let them. Instead, he took them by the hand and kissed them. Absalom did this with everyone who came to the king for judgment, and so he stole the hearts of all the people of Israel.

Do you see what is happening here? Absalom spent four years plotting and working to turn the hearts of the people of Israel away from his father, King David, and toward himself. Day after day, Absalom worked secretly to bring his father down. Absalom then came to David, stating that he needed to go to Hebron to offer sacrifices to the Lord. David agreed to let him go. We pick up the story in verse 10:

> But while he was there, he sent secret messengers to all the tribes of Israel to stir up a rebellion against the king.
> "As soon as you hear the ram's horn," his message read, "you are to say, 'Absalom has been crowned king in Hebron.'"
> He took two hundred men from Jerusalem with him as guests, but they knew nothing of his intentions. While Absalom was offering the sacrifices, he sent for Ahithophel, one of David's counselors who lived in Giloh. Soon, many others also joined Absalom, and the conspiracy gained momentum.

Even while Absalom was away, he continued to work to overthrow his father, David. In verse 13, David finally found out.

> A messenger soon arrived in Jerusalem to tell David, "All Israel has joined Absalom in a conspiracy against you!"
> "Then we must flee at once, or it will be too late!" David urged his men. "Hurry! If we get out of the city before Absalom arrives, both we and the city of Jerusalem will be spared from disaster."

When David found out about Absalom's plan, David made the difficult decision to flee Jerusalem rather than endure a bloody battle with his son. Why? Because even though Absalom had betrayed him,

David still loved his son and did not want to see him hurt or killed. In verse 23, we see true emotion come into the story as David and his followers make their way out of Jerusalem, escaping Absalom's soon-to-arrive army. "Everyone cried loudly as the king and his followers passed by. They crossed the Kidron Valley and then went out toward the wilderness."

Can you feel their emotion and pain? Notice it says, "They crossed the Kidron Valley." We will explore this more in-depth later. David was greatly affected by the rejection of Absalom. Verse 30 describes the rejection:

> David walked up the road to the Mount of Olives, weeping as he went. His head was covered, and his feet were bare as a sign of mourning. And the people who were with him covered their heads and wept as they climbed the hill.

David walked up the road weeping. Why? Because he had left his throne in Israel? No, because he had been rejected by his son Absalom. David felt so deeply the rejection a parent feels when their child betrays them. He was crushed by someone he loved greatly and who once loved him.

Many Bible scholars tell us that during David's escape from Absalom, he penned the words to his most well-known Psalm—Psalm 23. You see, David did not write Psalm 23 as he sat on the hillside tending his father's sheep on a beautiful sunny day. Instead, David wrote this psalm during one of the darkest times in his adult life. When David wrote in verse 4, "Yeah, though I walk through the valley of the shadow of death," he had *literally* walked through the valley of the shadow of death, the Kidron Valley; and he was *figuratively* walking through the valley of the shadow of death as he fled from Absalom and his army. However, David was also *emotionally* walking through the valley of the shadow of death as the pain from Absalom's rejection was so strong that David must have felt a part of his heart and soul die within him. He felt dead inside, and that may be the worst death of all. David had been rejected by someone he loved.

Rejection of a spouse

As Don got into his car and began the four-hour drive to his parents, the tears flowed as he poured his heart out to God. He knew things weren't right, but he did not realize his marriage was on the edge of the cliff. A thousand thoughts ran through his mind as he drove. What happened? What could I have done differently? Why didn't I see this coming? There were a lot of questions but very few answers.

For many of you, Don's story could have been called your story. Sure, the details are slightly different; maybe it was after a fight, or during a rough patch in the marriage, or even because of mistakes you made, but the story is pretty much the same. There was a point in time when your spouse decided they were no longer willing to continue their commitment for any number of reasons, and they were finished.

I believe the greatest rejection a human can endure is the rejection of a spouse. This is not said to downplay the rejection from a parent or child or any other relationship, but a couple differences make the pain of a spouse's rejection even worse. First, there is no other contract or covenant involving two people so public and personal. Each person takes a vow before God and man to be faithful to each other for life. The marriage vows are very straightforward and very specific.

> To have and to hold from this day forward.
> For better or for worse,
> For richer or for poorer,
> In sickness and in health,
> To love and to cherish,
> Till death do us part.

When another person vows to be with you in every situation, regardless of how good or bad things become, you take the first giant step toward becoming one.

Secondly, unlike any other relationship, you not only give your heart and mind to the other person, but you also commit your body to them as well. Mark 10:6–9 puts it like this:

> But at the beginning of creation God "made them male and female."
> "For this reason, a man will leave his father and mother and be united to his wife, and the two will become one flesh." So they are no longer two, but one flesh. Therefore, what God has joined together, let no one separate. (NIV)

The public commitment of faithfulness coupled with the private joining together sexually creates a strong bond between two people, unlike any other relationship. This bond should become stronger as the two become one flesh and begin doing life together. The "love" spoken of in a family relationship coupled with the "vulnerability" of letting another person into your innermost thoughts, dreams, weaknesses, feelings, faults, failures, and frustrations creates a bond that is meant to last a lifetime.

So what happens when that relationship begins to fall apart? Some have likened it to pulling apart two pieces of duct tape. The longer those pieces of duct tape are together, the more they melt into one piece. Can they be separated? Yes, but not without great effort and significant damage to both pieces of that tape. Just like the duct tape, marriage is meant to stay together. When pulled apart, there is substantial damage done to each spouse as well as the children involved, family, friends, and a host of others. Biblically speaking, one flesh is being ripped apart into two through a painful separation, one that was never intended to happen.

For the spouse that has been left at the altar, the rejection is more painful than words can describe. Susan put it like this, "It was probably the worst thing I had ever experienced because you think you are going to be sitting on the porch with your grandchildren years down the line, and then when you realize that it is suddenly cut short: you feel that very intensely." Make no mistake; however, while the other spouse may not feel rejection, the very fabric of who they once were is being ripped apart as well. Both parties will walk through the valley of divorce, even though their journeys will lead them down different paths with different feelings.

Where to go

In the post-separation world, an extraordinary phenomenon takes place. You are looking for stability from someone you trust, but the person you trusted the most betrayed your trust. You begin to look at others through a different lens. Can I trust that mutual friend? What does my church family think of me? Will my family be there to support me? The trust you once had has been broken, and you may find it difficult to trust even those closest to you. "I pulled away, and I internalized a lot," Beth recalled. "I just let very few people into my circle. I became more independent. I tried not to need people, so I couldn't get"—She paused—"left."

While most of our fears of rejection by our family, friends, and the church turn out to be unwarranted, there will be individuals that will reject you. Tami related, "I only had one friend that rejected me hugely. I still don't understand the why, but it happened."

Mark experienced more rejection. "There were some people that openly rejected me, and a few people pointedly rejected me. There were church people, not very many, but there were a few that rejected me."

Handling rejection

So how do you handle rejection? Possibly your story will be similar to Don's, who stated, "The only rejection I felt was from my former spouse." Remember, though, that Satan will try to get you to *believe* that everyone is rejecting you.

"Most of the rejection I felt was inside," stated Beth. You will probably experience that as well as being hypersensitive to every look, statement, and tone of voice of those who speak to you. While others may know you are hurting, few truly understand the right thing to say or do; therefore, they often say or do nothing.

In the beginning weeks and months after your separation, it is easy to be driven by your hurt. Remember the old saying, "hurt people hurt people." Whether you want to admit it or not, you are a hurt person, and it is extremely easy to lash out and hurt others during this time. Be very careful not to say or do something you will regret later.

The rejection of Jesus

Even Jesus experienced rejection during His time on earth. In fact, He experienced rejection greater than any of us will ever feel. John 1:11 reads, "He came to his own people, and even they *rejected* him" (NLT). Again, the greatest pain comes from those you love the most. Jesus was rejected by "His own people." These were the ones that were supposed to love and accept Christ, but instead, they rejected Him.

Jesus also experienced the rejection of the church.

> "The Son of Man must suffer many terrible things," He said. "He will be *rejected* by the elders, the leading priests, and the teachers of religious law. He will be killed, but on the third day, he will be raised from the dead." (Luke 9:22 NLT)

Those who should have recognized Jesus rejected Him instead. Because of that rejection, Jesus was sentenced to die by crucifixion.

Jesus has felt the awful sting of rejection. He was rejected by his entire generation.[6] He knows the pain you are feeling, and He has walked in your shoes and is always present to help you during times of trouble.[7] Jesus has been through the valley of rejection.

Conclusion

So how do you handle that rejection? "I cried a lot," Don said. "There was a lot of prayer." You have been hurt, and the healing will

---

[6] Luke 17:25
[7] Psalm 46:1

only begin once the hurt is recognized and dealt with. When the tears come, don't fight them. However, when you cry, cry out to Jesus. Tell Him about the pain you are feeling. He knows how that pain feels. There was one other thing that Don did at the advice of a friend. He worshiped. He sang songs; he praised God. He put his mind in an attitude of worship. We will discuss this more later on. You must realize at the beginning that during this process, your greatest enemy will not be your ex-spouse but rather your mind. Focus your mind on the One who "will never leave you nor forsake you,[8]" and you have taken the first step in overcoming the excruciating pain of rejection.

Psalm 23 (King James Version)

> The LORD is my shepherd; I shall not want.
> He maketh me to lie down in green pastures: He leadeth me beside the still waters.
> He restoreth my soul: He leadeth me in the paths of righteousness for His name's sake.
> Yea, though I walk through the valley of the shadow of death, I will fear no evil: for Thou art with me; thy rod and thy staff they comfort me.
> Thou preparest a table before me in the presence of mine enemies: thou anointest my head with oil; my cup runneth over.
> Surely goodness and mercy shall follow me all the days of my life: and I will dwell in the house of the LORD forever.

---

[8] Hebrews 13:5

Chapter 2

Dark Days

I spent every morning facedown, praying and begging God to help me get up and do what I had to do. I didn't think it would ever end.

—Tami

It was truly the darkest days of my life.

—Susan

Why am I discouraged? Why is my heart so sad?
I will put my hope in God! I will praise him again—
my Savior and my God!

—Psalm 42:5–6a NLT

Susan's story

Susan had been married for twenty-six years. She planned to be with her husband for the rest of her life. Her life plans changed the day Susan discovered that she had been betrayed by the man she loved. After her husband walked out of the door for the last time, Susan made her way to the bedroom, lied down on his side of the bed, and "cried and cried and cried." Years later, she still recalls how the pillow and sheet had the smell of her husband that day. The marriage was over, but the crying had just begun.

Susan was experiencing the first of many dark days to come. She was taking the beginning steps into the valley of divorce, and the next few months would be filled with some of the darkest days she would ever endure. Everyone who has walked through the valley of divorce has a story to tell, and every story includes a darkness, potentially overwhelming at times.

Everyone has a story

Alissa recalled this time in her own life. "I just survived. I remember just getting up, and I was in a fog. I was just doing it. I would get my girl ready and get her to the babysitter. I would go into work and help, and the whole time I just felt dead, death. I felt nothing. I would cry sometimes. It was like a death inside. It was like black, hanging, oppressing, and I wanted light."

My story is somewhat similar. I remember thinking, *If I can just make it through the next six months, everything will begin to get better.* I had the foresight to look ahead to a brighter time, but I didn't know how to make it through the next week or even the next day. It is a very difficult time. You don't want to be alone, but you don't want anyone around. You need to be out doing things, but you don't really want to do anything. Nothing really sounds fun or enjoyable. All you can see is the darkness that lies ahead while currently the darkness also envelops you.

Tami relates how she would "lay facedown on the floor, praying and begging God to 'help me go, help me go.' I just didn't feel like I could go. I felt like the whole world was on my shoulders. I would have never gotten out of my bed if I didn't have my kids. I had to get up because I had little kids." Thinking back on that time, she said, "It looked like it was never going to end."

King David's dark days

In the previous chapter, we left King David as he was fleeing from his son Absalom, who sought to overthrow his father's throne. 2 Samuel 15:30 reads:

> David walked up the road to the Mount of Olives, weeping as he went. His head was covered, and his feet were bare as a sign of mourning. And the people who were with him covered their heads and wept as they climbed the hill. (NLT)

David was experiencing the first of many dark days to follow. In addition, there is one crucial point that requires notice. David had just walked through the Kidron Valley and was now making his way up the Mount of Olives. Please don't overlook this critical fact. To get out of the valley, you will have to begin climbing up the mountain. The very definition of a valley is "a low area between hills or mountains." To get out, you have to progress upward. Unlike David, you will not reach the top of the mountain in one day. Climbing out of the valley is a process including good days of progress and bad days of decline. The goal, though, is to keep moving in the right direction. We will look at this more in-depth in chapter 15.

In the next verse (31), as David is climbing up the Mount of Olives, he receives news that his advisor, Ahithophel, is now backing Absalom. David's climb up the mountain was interrupted by a setback; he had lost someone he thought he could trust. However, David continued his journey, and in verse 32, he reached the top of the Mount of Olives. He had successfully escaped out of Jerusalem and out of sight of Absalom and his soon-to-arrive army, but unfortunately, David's battle was far from over.

The next step

As Susan's tears began to subside, she got up from the bed, "ripped the sheets off, and did the laundry." Susan didn't get rid of the sheets, but she did get rid of the scent acting as a constant reminder of her loss. Many more things would be removed to ease the pain during difficult days.

For Alissa, a more aggressive approach was enacted. The darkness she felt was because of the separation and the drugs, alcohol, abuse, and other evils brought into the marriage. "I started through the house. If I found a sock of his, I would burn it or get rid of it. I wanted everything out. That was the start of my process of removing the darkness. I would search from the top of the house to the bottom of the house for anything that was his, and I would get rid of it." Alissa went as far as putting in new carpet and painting the walls a lighter and brighter color. All of this represented newness, and with each step came a little bit of healing and a little more peace.

During the dark days of divorce, you will often be acting on emotion or instinct. Test yourself and your thoughts. Are they true? Are you being honest with yourself? Check your actions. Are you getting rid of this out of spite, or is this a necessary step in healing? Will you regret this decision later on?

Also, look past the immediate. You are on a journey. You will not completely heal in one day, but you can take a step or two or three in the right direction each day. After a while, you will be able to look back and see how far you've come.

Christ's darkest hour

Remember, everyone goes through difficult times and dark days. Jesus Christ was no exception. In Luke 22:14–20, we find the story of Jesus and His disciples sitting down to eat the Passover meal. Passover was a time of joy, but Jesus was very serious. As everyone else began to celebrate, Jesus's mind was fixed on the horrible things that He knew He was going to have to endure over the next twenty-four hours.

> When the time came, Jesus and the apostles
> sat down together at the table.

> Jesus said, "I have been very eager to eat this Passover meal with you before my suffering begins. For I tell you now that I won't eat this meal again until its meaning is fulfilled in the Kingdom of God." Then he took a cup of wine and gave thanks to God for it. Then he said, "Take this and share it among yourselves. For I will not drink wine again until the Kingdom of God has come." He took some bread and gave thanks to God for it. Then he broke it in pieces and gave it to the disciples, saying, "This is my body, which is given for you. Do this in remembrance of me."
>
> After supper, He took another cup of wine and said, "This cup is the new covenant between God and His people—an agreement confirmed with my blood, which is poured out as a sacrifice for you."

Jesus was focused on the future, even though everyone around him was living in the moment. Only Jesus knew that He was sitting down to what we know today as "the Last Supper."

Even though the event was a happy one, Jesus could feel the darkness of evil closing in around Him. Before the night was over, He would be betrayed, beaten, falsely accused, and sentenced to die for sins He had never committed. His body was about to be broken, and His blood was about to be shed. That Last Supper was truly the beginning of Christ's darkest hours of His life on earth.

Conclusion

Knowing Jesus has experienced times far darker than you, or I will ever go through, should lead you closer to Him. For Susan, this proved true. "I started filling every part of my life with Christian music. I had the radio on K-Love 24-7. If I got up in the middle of the night to get a drink of water, there would be a song playing, and almost every time, it would be a song that was truly speaking to me. I left the radio on in my bedroom," Susan recalled. "I would start just copying down Scripture. I felt like I had gone ankle-deep with God before. During that time, I was neck-, nose-, and forehead- deep with God."

Susan had lost her spouse of twenty-six years, but she chose to immerse herself in a deeper relationship with God. As you traverse through the valley of divorce, you will experience many dark days. However, you do not have to walk the road alone. Your time spent in the valley can be a time of refreshing and renewal with God. When this happens, you can find peace even during the darkest days, and you can begin your climb out of the valley and toward the mountaintop. Dark days will not last forever, and the sun will shine again, even though you "walk through the valley."

Psalm 23 (New Living Translation): A psalm of David

> The LORD is my shepherd; I have all that I need.
>
> He lets me rest in green meadows; He leads me beside peaceful streams.
>
> He renews my strength. He guides me along right paths, bringing honor to His name.
>
> Even when I walk through the darkest valley, I will not be afraid, for You are close beside me. Your rod and Your staff protect and comfort me.
>
> You prepare a feast for me in the presence of my enemies.
>
> You honor me by anointing my head with oil. My cup overflows with blessings.
>
> Surely your goodness and unfailing love will pursue me all the days of my life, and I will live in the house of the LORD forever.

Emotional Exhaustion

> My exhaustion was more due to the haunting images of thinking about what was going on.
>
> —Don

> I struggled for years. I still have battle scars.
>
> —Beth

> *But those who trust in the L*ORD *will find new strength.*
> *They will soar high on wings like eagles.*
> *They will run and not grow weary.*
> *They will walk and not faint.*
>
> —Isaiah 40:31 KJV

Tami's story

Tami's marriage was over, but her life had to go on. She had two small children who were relying on her for their needs. However, Tami had no energy. She was emotionally exhausted. "I coped," she recalled, "nothing was positive. I was just coping." Tami would go to work, come home, fix dinner for her children, and then sit in their big oversized living room chair. One child would squeeze in on the right and one on the left, and they would spend the evening staring at the TV until bedtime. "They thought it was grand. I was just coping. I didn't have the energy to be with them or do anything. All my energy went into just getting through."

Don tells a similar story. "I found out early on, every other night, I couldn't sleep." Don would spend one night tossing and turning as his mind was fixed on what was going on. "The next day, I would have to get up and go to work. I would be exhausted physically by the end of the day, and I would crash as soon as I got home, and I would sleep all night long." This two-day cycle continued over and over again.

Proper energy distribution

This emotional exhaustion is pervasive while walking through this dark valley of divorce. In fact, fatigue during divorce is easily explained. When you are balanced and simply living your day-to-day life, your energy is somewhat equally split into four areas: spiritual, physical, mental, and emotional energy. You may have a physically exhausting day that requires energy to be borrowed from the other three, but you will quickly return to normal. You may be finishing up a big presentation at work, and your mental side will require more energy; but again, you will quickly come back into balance.

However, during a separation and divorce, your emotional energy will often require as much as 85 percent of your body's energy supply, thus leaving only 15 percent to be divided between your spiritual, physical, and mental energy.[9] Therefore, divorce leaves you feeling physically, mentally, and spiritually depleted as if there is virtually no energy left to meet the demands. Combine this with difficulty sleeping at night, and you can quickly relate with Alissa when she recalled, "I was a walking zombie."

---

[9] www.divorcecare.org

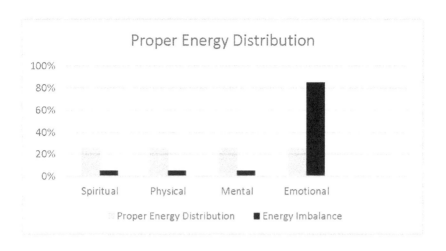

To this point, you may not have been able to understand why you always felt so tired. What you are feeling is something almost everyone experiences as they grapple with divorce. You probably feel like Tami, who related, "I had no energy for anything else except what had to be done."

King David's emotional exhaustion

When we last left King David, he had escaped from Jerusalem shortly before Absalom and his army had arrived. David is now on the top of the Mount of Olives, "where people worshiped God,"[10] but the Bible doesn't talk about David worshiping. Maybe he did, but likely his energy was so heavily consumed by his emotional, mental, and physical demands that David had zero energy left for the spiritual. By this point, David is suffering from physical exhaustion as he has traversed up the Mount of Olives from the Kidron Valley below. David is experiencing overwhelming emotional fatigue as he has wept while reeling from his son's rejection. David is mentally drained as his mind tries to process the events of the last few hours. Although literally on the top of the mountain, David's journey will take him deep into the wilderness.

---

[10] 2 Samuel 15:32b

In 2 Samuel 16, we pick up the story as David and his followers descend the backside of the Mount of Olives and continue their escape into the wilderness. At this point, David has to be totally drained in every aspect of his being. His dark day, however, holds one more undesired surprise. The story is told beginning with verse 5:

> As King David came to Bahurim, a man came out of the village cursing them. It was Shimei, son of Gera, from the same clan as Saul's family. He threw stones at the king and the king's officers and all the mighty warriors who surrounded him.
>
> "Get out of here, you murderer, you scoundrel!" he shouted at David. "The LORD is paying you back for all the bloodshed in Saul's clan. You stole his throne, and now the LORD has given it to your son Absalom. At last, you will taste some of your own medicine for you are a murderer!"

Just when it seemed things couldn't get any worse, David finds himself on the receiving end of an angry man throwing stones at David and cursing him and calling him a murderer. We pick up the story in verse 9:

> "Why should this dead dog curse my lord the king?" Abishai, son of Zeruiah, demanded. "Let me go over and cut off his head!"
>
> "No!" the king said. "Who asked your opinion, you sons of Zeruiah! If the LORD has told him to curse me, who are you to stop Him?"
>
> Then David said to Abishai and to all his servants, "My own son is trying to kill me. Doesn't this relative of Saul have even more reason to do so? Leave him alone and let him curse, for the LORD has told him to do it. And perhaps

> the LORD will see that I am being wronged and will bless me because of these curses today."

David's response, or lack thereof, shows just how utterly drained he was. David could have shouted back at Shimei or told Abishai to kill him, but David simply chose to do nothing. David, the king and a mighty warrior, does not have the energy or will to deal with one malicious man. The story continues:

> So David and his men continued down the road, and Shimei kept pace with them on a nearby hillside, cursing and throwing stones and dirt at David. The king and all who were with him grew weary along the way, so they rested when they reached the Jordan River.

As David continued on his way, Shimei continued cursing David and throwing stones and dirt at him. Finally, the Bible says what we could have all expected, "the king and all who were with him grew weary." This day had taken every last bit of spiritual, emotional, mental, and physical energy from David. There was nothing left to do but rest.

Christ faced emotional exhaustion

Emotional exhaustion happens to everyone at some point. Even Christ faced it as He looked ahead to what He was about to endure. After the Last Supper, "accompanied by the disciples, Jesus left the upstairs room and went as usual to the Mount of Olives" (Luke 22:39). Do you see it? Are you connecting the dots? Jesus walked the same route as David did during David's darkest day! Jesus walked out of Jerusalem through the Kidron Valley and on to the Mount of Olives. During Jesus's darkest hour, we find Him in the Garden of Gethsemane on the Mount of Olives.

Continuing with verse 40,

> There he told them, "Pray that you will not give in to temptation."
> He walked away, about a stone's throw, and knelt down and prayed, "Father, if you are willing, please take this cup of suffering away from me. Yet I want your will to be done, not mine."
> Then an angel from heaven appeared and strengthened him. He prayed more fervently, and He was in such agony of spirit that His sweat fell to the ground like great drops of blood.

Jesus's emotional exhaustion was so great that God sent an angel from heaven to strengthen Him. The sent angel didn't fix all of the problems Jesus was facing but gave Jesus some added strength to make it to the cross. Notice the wordage used in verse 44. It states that Jesus was in "such agony of spirit." What is agony of spirit? It can be described as mental and emotional exhaustion. In fact, the Bible describes Jesus's distress in detail, "His sweat fell to the ground like great drops of blood." In recent years, a name has been put to this condition. It is called "hematohidrosis," which occurs in individuals who are "suffering from extreme levels of stress."[11] Jesus was under such emotional stress and anguish that he literally began sweating blood. Therefore, when we are going through difficult times, it is helpful to realize Jesus truly understands the extreme stress and anguish we are experiencing because He also experienced it.

Emotional exhaustion is real. If you are in the darkest part of the valley of divorce, you will, in all likelihood, experience it. So what can be done about it? Let's look at the next two verses, Luke 22:45–46:

---

[11] www.ncbi.nlm.nih.gov

> At last he stood up again and returned to the disciples, only to find them asleep, exhausted from grief.
>
> "Why are you sleeping?" he asked them. "Get up and pray, so that you will not give in to temptation."

Jesus returned to the disciples and found them asleep. Why? They were "exhausted from grief." Even the disciples were experiencing emotional exhaustion. In verse 46, Jesus gives them the answer to overcoming emotional exhaustion. "Why are you sleeping?" He asked them. "Get up and pray so that you will not give in to temptation." So prayer is the answer? How can that be?

Conclusion

Beth said, "Spiritually, I became closer to God during this time." When you are exhausted, down, and defeated, you are a prime target of Satan. This is the time when you need to pray most. If you don't pray to God, Satan will most definitely prey on you. However, it goes even a little deeper. Your mental and emotional energy comes directly from your mind. If your mind is in turmoil, you are going to be mentally and emotionally exhausted. However, even though your world and situation might be in shambles, if your mind is at peace, your emotions will also subside. So how do you put your mind at peace? You do so by devoting more energy to your physical and spiritual side. Don't misunderstand me. This is not an overnight fix, but science explains that exercise helps to settle the mind. However, true and lasting peace can only come from one source and the source is God.

Don knows this well. During his darkest days, following a counselor's advice, Don directed his energy toward the spiritual. He began to worship and draw closer to God even though he felt like doing nothing. What happened? "It built my optimism, my faith, my sense of purpose that God's not done with me yet." By upping his spiritual energy, his emotional and mental energy began to level out.

Do not feel ashamed when you find yourself emotionally exhausted; I have been there. Those I interviewed have been there. Even King David, Jesus, and His disciples have experienced this exhaustion. Get the rest you need. Force yourself to get some exercise, and most of all, worship God and pray to Him while you lay your burdens at His feet. The peace of mind given only by God is what will help you overcome this very real battle.

Then Jesus said, "Come to me, all of *you* who are weary and carry heavy burdens, and *I will give you rest*" (Matthew 11:28).

Psalm 23 (Good News Translation): The Lord, our Shepherd

> The LORD is my shepherd; I have everything I need.
>
> He lets me rest in fields of green grass and leads me to quiet pools of fresh water.
>
> He gives me new strength. He guides me in the right paths, as He has promised.
>
> Even if I go through the deepest darkness, I will not be afraid, LORD, for You are with me.
>
> Your shepherd's rod and staff protect me.
>
> You prepare a banquet for me, where all my enemies can see me; You welcome me as an honored guest and fill my cup to the brim.
>
> I know that your goodness and love will be with me all my life; and your house will be my home as long as I live.

Chapter 4

Shame

> The shame came from the idea that, at least for my part, I had allowed the disconnect to happen, and didn't recognize it as it was happening.
>
> —Mark

> I didn't feel shame until after things had calmed down—maybe a year later—and then shame set in, but that's because I did wrong. I made the wrong choice; I broke my vows. All of that brings much shame that I'll never get past.
>
> —Tami

> *In You, O Lord, I put my trust;*
> *Let me never be put to shame.*
>
> —Psalm 71:1 NKJV

Alissa's story

It had been about six months since Alissa's divorce had been finalized. However, she was still living in shame. For her, it seemed as if she had "a big *D* tattooed" on her chest that stood for "divorced." It was dictating who she was and limiting who she could become.

On this particular day, Alissa had dropped off her little girl with the babysitter and was driving a back road to work. The shame was overwhelming. Finally, Alissa stopped the car in the middle of the road and began to weep. She felt so ashamed. This wasn't how her story was supposed to go.

Defining shame

We often speak of shame, but what is it? Webster defines it as "a painful feeling of humiliation or distress caused by the consciousness of wrong or foolish behavior." However, sometimes that feeling of shame comes, as in Alissa's story, not because of what we have done, but rather because of the position in life in which we find ourselves. Alissa was ashamed not because of her actions but rather because she was the victim of an abusive and ultimately a failed marriage. She was ashamed because she was "divorced," even though she did everything she could to save the marriage.

The shame that we feel "makes us direct our focus inward and view our entire self in a negative light. Feelings of guilt, in contrast, result from a concrete action for which we accept responsibility. Guilt causes us to focus our attention on the feelings of others."[12] What are you feeling? Are you experiencing guilt because of your words or actions, or are you experiencing shame because of your situation? That is the big problem with shame—we begin to be consumed with everything negative about ourselves, and Satan can use that negative intrinsic thinking to drive us deeper and deeper into self-loathing, doubts, and depression.

Tami illustrated the dangers of such thinking when she reflected on her shameful feelings after the end of her second marriage. "I shouldn't have felt shame. I don't suppose because I didn't do anything wrong, but I just felt so ashamed that I had a second failed marriage and that I couldn't somehow succeed," she said as she pondered the past. "Then I decided, 'I must not be marriage material.

---

[12] https://www.scientificamerican.com/article/the-scientific-underpinnings-and-impacts-of-shame/

I'm not meant for marriage. I'm not a good wife,' you know, all that." Can you see the negative intrinsic thinking spiraling downward?

It has been said that "we feel shame when we violate the social norms we believe in."[13] For someone like Tami or Alissa, that feeling is exacerbated when one has been raised in a Christian home where divorce violates the "social norms" in which we believe. Do not misunderstand; growing up in a stable, Christian home is a huge blessing, but watching your marriage fall apart when you have grown up watching a successful marriage lived out before you can lead to tremendous feelings of shame and failure. Mark stated, "I think I felt a profound feeling of failure. I didn't like that." Similarly, Beth recalls, "I'm a person that is not wired to fail, and I was a fool or made a fool of. I felt like I was an idiot." That feeling of failure can produce great shame.

Proper shame

Not all shame is bad if that shame is a driving force that leads to repentance. Again, looking at the life of David, we find a great example of this. It had been a year since King David committed adultery with Bathsheba. However, this sin was still hidden. The Prophet Nathan comes to David and brings this sin into the light. In Psalm 51, we see David turning that guilt and shame into a prayer of repentance.

> Have mercy on me, O God,
> because of your unfailing love.
> Because of your great compassion,
> blot out the stain of my sins.
> Wash me clean from my guilt.
> Purify me from my sin.
> For I recognize my rebellion;
> it haunts me day and night.
> Against You, and You alone, have I sinned;
> I have done what is evil in your sight.

---

[13] https://www.scientificamerican.com/article/the-scientific-underpinnings-and-impacts-of-shame/

Can you see the intrinsic thinking as David confesses his sin to God and asks for forgiveness? Look again at verse 3, "For I recognize my rebellion; it haunts me day and night." For a year, David had been haunted by the sin he had committed with Bathsheba. Now we see David confess his sin. His shame is leading to repentance. We continue with verse 7:

> Purify me from my sins, and I will be clean;
> wash me, and I will be whiter than snow.
> Oh, give me back my joy again;
> you have broken me—
> now let me rejoice.
> Don't keep looking at my sins.
> Remove the stain of my guilt.
> Create in me a clean heart, O God.
> Renew a loyal spirit within me. (NLT)

David was ashamed of his sin, but he made the decision to no longer live with that shame. His appropriate response allowed David to be restored to a proper place in the eyes of God. If your shame is based upon mistakes you made in the marriage that caused it to fall apart, that shame is appropriate. However, that shame will either drive you to repentance or will drive you down a deep and dark road. Your shame must be properly dealt with or it will act as a wall that will greatly hinder you in your healing journey.

The shame of the Cross

We know that Jesus felt the sting of rejection, experienced dark days, and endured emotional exhaustion. Surely, He didn't feel shame, right? After all, Jesus never made a mistake or committed a sin, so what could He possibly have to be ashamed of? In Hebrews 12, we see the author encouraging us to "run the race" successfully. How? In verse 2 we read:

> We do this by keeping our eyes on Jesus, the
> champion who initiates and perfects our faith.-

> Because of the joy awaiting Him, He endured the cross, *disregarding its shame*. Now He is seated in the place of honor beside God's throne. (NLT)

Did you see it? Jesus disregarded or "despised" (KJV) the shame of the cross. What shame was this? To quote John Piper, "Shame was stripping away every earthly support that Jesus had: his friends gave way in shaming abandonment; his reputation gave way in shaming mockery; his decency gave way in shaming nakedness; his comfort gave way in shaming torture. His glorious dignity gave way to the utterly undignified, degrading reflexes of grunting and groaning and screeching."[14]

Jesus felt great shame. However, it should be noted that none of this shame was caused by any sin or mistake of Jesus. It was all because of the situation that Jesus was in. He was not responsible for the shame, but yet He experienced it. What is the reason for your shame? Is it because you did wrong, is it because you are divorced, a single parent, or because your life is currently a mess, even though you have done all you can to prevent it? If your shame is caused by your situation, your response should mirror that of Christ.

Jesus was experiencing the shame of abandonment, mockery, nakedness, torture, and the Cross; but Jesus "disregarded" this shame. Jesus looked past the Cross to the joy that awaited Him and mankind and willingly walked through the valley lined with shame. He refused to let the shame define Him and, "now He is seated in the place of honor beside God's throne."

Conclusion

As Alissa sat weeping in her car in the middle of the road, her weeping was interrupted by the clear voice of the Holy Spirit saying "STOP, STOP. I need you to tell my daughters to STOP living in shame and bondage from being divorced. They are not living their life to the fullest. Literally, shame has bogged them down. Whether it was

---

[14] https://www.desiringgod.org/articles/what-does-it-mean-for-jesus-to-despise-shame

their fault or not is irrelevant. Tell my daughters they can be used. I still have a plan."

The tears that Alissa shed were replaced with a peace that only God can give. "My calling has always been to help other people through my experiences," Alissa said, and now she realized that God was going to use her experience and her story to help other ladies who would walk the same dark road. She had been controlled by her shame, but God wanted her to comfort others by her story.

What's your story? Does it include shame? Is that shame valid? If so, what do you need to do to overcome it? If not, how long will you let it define you? You are not defined by your past. You are not defined by your situation. You are not defined by others. You are not defined by that figurative *D* on your chest. You are defined by who you are now and who you will become. If you have shame, it is time to deal with it or disregard it. You must move past it and not let it define you. Let God take your shame and turn your story into history, better yet, let God turn your story into His-story. There is no shame in that.

Psalm 23 (English Standard Version): The L ORD *is my Shepherd, a psalm of David*

> The LORD is my shepherd; I shall not want.
> He makes me lie down in green pastures. He leads me beside still waters.
> He restores my soul. He leads me in paths of righteousness for his name's sake.
> Even though I walk through the valley of the shadow of death, I will fear no evil,
> for You are with me; your rod and your staff, they comfort me.
> You prepare a table before me in the presence of my enemies; You anoint my head with oil; my cup overflows.
> Surely goodness and mercy shall follow me all the days of my life, and I shall dwell in the house of the LORD forever.

CHAPTER 5

Triggers

> Things left in the dark have power
> over you; but when you put them in
> the light, they lose their power.
>
> —Alissa

> When people's voices raise or there is tension,
> I am immediately triggered. I will almost
> cry. I will tell myself, "They aren't going
> to hit me. I'm not going to be hurt."
>
> —Tami

> *For I know the thoughts that I think*
> *toward you, says the L*ORD*,*
> *thoughts of peace and not of evil,*
> *to give you a future and a hope.*
>
> —*Jeremiah 29:11 KJV*

Tami's story

It had been a little under a year since Tami's ex-husband had left. It had been a marriage filled with verbal and physical abuse. Even though time had passed, the scars and memories lived on and bad feelings were easily triggered by situations that didn't pose a threat.

Tami had been wanting to build a loft bed for her son in his room, and this seemed to be the perfect time to start the project as her son was out of town for the weekend. Tami contacted her friend (we will call him Steven) and employed him to help with this task. Steven was in his twenties and was "a very kind, gentle, and quiet man. You wouldn't meet a sweeter man," Tami commented.

Tami and Steven went and got the plans and lumber for the bed. Steven loved these kinds of projects, and he was excited to begin building. When they returned back to the house, Steven began looking at the plans, then the lumber, then he "jumped up" and walked quickly into the bedroom. He then quickly returned and again looked at the plans, looked at the lumber, and jumped up and headed back into the bedroom. He was zoned in, and he was excited. This process was repeated several times. While Steven was concentrating on the project, Tami was watching Steven as he intensely made laps between the plans and the space where the bed would go. This intensity coming from an unsuspecting Steven was triggering an unsolicited reaction from Tami. "My heart started racing," Tami recalled.

She finally told Steven, "Now listen, we don't have to do this, it's okay."

Steven stopped what he was working on, looked up at Tami in confusion, and questioned, "You don't want the bed?"

Tami did want the bed, but she didn't want the feelings that were boiling up inside of her. The intensity and pacing from her friend Steven was causing Tami to be triggered. She tried to diffuse the situation she perceived as dangerous because her mind had quickly raced back to the many times during her marriage where a tense situation like this would result in Tami being physically or verbally abused. She was absolutely in no danger this time, but her mind still perceived the excitement and intensity as a threat and triggered certain reactions in her body such as increased heart rate, tension, and feelings of stress.

Understanding the mind

Triggers will happen after any relationship, abusive or not, but in order to understand why they happen, we must first understand how our minds work. Inside the head of every human being rests the greatest computer ever invented. In fact, your brain is thirty times faster than the best supercomputer.[15] Your mind is receiving signals from all over your body at speeds well above any speed limit in the United States. It is amazing, but it is not without fault.

When you are born, your brain is like a sponge waiting to be filled with information. Your environment and experiences begin to take that sponge and form it. When an experience happens over and over, your brain builds a "shortcut" reaction to that experience. Maybe you remember studying about "Pavlov's dog" during your high school or college psychology class. If not, here is a little refresher.

Pavlov discovered that his dog would salivate whenever he brought food to the canine. Over time, Pavlov added the ringing of a bell each time he brought his dog food. Again, the dog would salivate as he came for his food. Then Pavlov stopped bringing the food and simply rang the bell. Even though there was no food, the dog would still salivate when he heard the bell. Why? Because the dog's brain had been trained to connect the bell with food, and food brought about involuntary salivating from the dog. Pavlov's experiment proved that "unrelated behaviors can trigger similar responses." The conditioned stimulus brought about an unconditioned response.[16]

Now, let's relate this back to Tami's experience. For years, Tami's mind had experienced a high-intensity situation followed by physical or verbal abuse. Her mind had created a "shortcut." In her mind, if *A* (intense situation) happened, then *B* (abuse) would also happen. Her body, in anticipation of *B* happening, reacted with increased heartbeat, stress, fear, and a last-ditch effort to diffuse the situation. Even after many years, Tami's mind still perceived threats where no threat existed, and these perceived threats led to triggers like increased heartbeat, fear, and other responses.

---

[15] https://spectrum.ieee.org/tech-talk/computing/networks/estimate-human-brain-30-times-faster-than-best-supercomputers

[16] https://www.youtube.com/watch?v=-XttvR7NxHw

Other triggers

Not all marriages end because of abuse. However, a failed marriage and separation from your "other half" will most definitely bring about triggers. These triggers can occur when you least expect them. Triggers cause an emotion within you or a reaction from you. Even though your former spouse may be hundreds or thousands of miles away, you will still experience things that will remind you of him/her. It may be a smell, an event, a picture, a significant date (like an anniversary or birthday), a place, furniture; and the list goes on and on.

What makes triggers so difficult is often the response they elicit. Mark recalls, "an icy feeling in the pit of my stomach. It was hard to breathe." Don describes his reaction to triggers as "a sick feeling in the gut. A sense of disgust. When I was passing certain places, it was like a train wreck or a car wreck. You want to look, but you don't want to look. Many times, there were tears. The pain, you know, that sorrow and grief in your heart—that brokenness lasts for a while."

Living with triggers

While we all wish triggers would just go away, that will never totally be the case. However, it does get better. Mark remarks, "With each progressive year that goes by, there are fewer triggers." Don simply said, "I don't think about her anymore. I just don't. I'm past it." Even in the case of Tami, that "fight-or-flight" reaction of the mind brought about by years of abuse will lessen with time. However, when one's mind has been changed by abuse and trauma, it will have to be retrained in order to create new paths which lead to new responses.

One of the biggest mistakes one can make in dealing with triggers is to simply avoid them. This reaction only causes the pain brought on by triggers to linger and the healing to be put on hold. Susan recalls one such event in her story. While married, Susan and her husband would often go to Jose Peppers. Soon after the divorce, a friend asked Susan to go to Jose Peppers.

"I don't know if I can," Susan said.

Her friend responded, "Don't you want to make new memories?"

Susan exclaimed, "Yes!"

From that time on, she began combating triggers by replacing them with new memories. When you experience a trigger, "you lean into the moment and then you let it go," says Susan.

Overcoming triggers

"I've learned when triggers happen, not to negate them and push them down, and act like they didn't happen. I've begun to explore them," relates Alissa. "One thing I told myself is that I will feel everything. I made myself promise that I will walk through it. I will not try to go around it, underneath it, or over it, and if I do, I'm going to make myself go back. I am going to walk it: every emotion, anger, guilt, doubt, fear, regret. I'm going to feel it all because I want to use this to further the kingdom. I want to be healthy. I want to be whole."

It all boils down to this: You can choose to avoid all those places and memories that trigger you, but you are simply preventing yourself from healing. Susan recalls the day when her husband left and she knew divorce was inevitable. As she sat on the floor beside her bed, she told herself, "This will make me bitter, or this will make me better." At that moment, Susan chose to become better. Each of us has a choice to make. Will this experience destroy us or will we choose to learn from it and become stronger?

Remember that memories, while they will fade with time, will never completely go away. Triggers, while they will subside, will continue. You, however, choose how to react when they come. As for Alissa, she was determined to face those memories head-on. "With a trigger, as it comes, I explore it. I let myself feel it and remember it and then just let it go because it's no longer my present. That was my past."

One of the early indications of your healing will be when you begin to look toward your future, rather than living in the past. It won't happen overnight, but it will happen. Just remember, when you can, move on. As the famous quote by Mary Englebreit states, "Don't look back—you're not going that way." You have a future; don't let it be dictated by the past.

Psalm 23 (World English Bible): A psalm by David

Yahweh is my shepherd: I shall lack nothing.

He makes me lie down in green pastures. He leads me beside still waters.

He restores my soul. He guides me in the paths of righteousness for His name's sake.

Even though I walk through the valley of the shadow of death, I will fear no evil, for You are with me. Your rod and your staff, they comfort me.

You prepare a table before me in the presence of my enemies.

You anoint my head with oil. My cup runs over.

Surely goodness and loving kindness shall follow me all the days of my life, and I will dwell in Yahweh's house forever.

SECTION 2

The Cry for Help

> I held everything in. I hadn't told my parents anything until the day he left. I really didn't open up to people at all. I just had a general mistrust of people at that point and I thought, *If I don't open up to people, I can't get burned.*
>
> —Beth

> *But in my distress, I cried out to the L<small>ORD</small>;*
> *yes, I cried to my God for help.*
> *He heard me from His sanctuary;*
> *my cry reached His ears.*
>
> —*2 Samuel 22:7 NLT*

The cry for help

The once-active house now falls eerily silent. Things are not quiet, however, not in the least. Inside your head are a thousand voices, memories, regrets, wishes, and fears, all converging as they fight to be the one to grasp your attention. Even though one could hear a pin drop around you, inside your head the noise and confusion would rival Times Square on New Year's Eve. "What just happened? How did this happen? What do I do now?" The questions seem to be lined up as far as the eye can see, but the answers are nowhere to be found.

Then come the voices of self-doubt. "I can't do this on my own. I'm not good enough to be loved by someone else. I tried and I failed. That makes me an epic failure." Your mind quickly races back to when it all began. Things were so perfect then. "He/she was the one I had sought after all my life. What happened? How did we go from a beautiful 'I do' on our wedding day to 'I don't want to see you again' today? Should I have done things differently? What could I have done?"

Perhaps in an instant, your mind makes another leap. You are transformed out of the past and into the present and future. Who do you call first? As you pick up the phone and begin to dial, you know you are getting ready to drop a bombshell on the person at the other end of the line. How do you tell others you love your marriage is over? This doesn't just affect you. Oh, no. This news will spread like the shock waves of an earthquake, and those shock waves will knock many to their knees.

Some will rush to your aid like a medic to a wounded soldier on the battlefield. Others you counted as faithful friends and relatives will turn their backs or at least stay standing in the shadows. Can there be a worse feeling in the world than this? *When will these voices in my head subside?* you wonder. You have been thrust into a dark and scary valley. You feel so alone but don't know where to go or who to turn to.

There is only one thing to do. You must make yourself vulnerable and cry for help.

Chapter 6

Loneliness

> Nighttime was horrible. When I laid down to sleep, it was horrible.
>
> —Don

> I had never lived by myself, so I had to face a house where you hear noises at night.
>
> —Susan

> *What time I am afraid, I will trust in thee.*
>
> —Psalm 56:3 NLT

My (Tim's) story

It had been three months since my wife left. I was managing to keep my head above water, but that was about it. I came home from work on a Friday night. I was worn out, like every night, since I was suffering from emotional exhaustion. I took a nap to refresh. About that time, my mind started thinking about the weekend now at my doorstep. Then I realized it, and the thought of it horrified me.

At any other point in my life, the thought would have brought about joy and excitement, but not at the stage I found myself in. I came to the realization I had absolutely nothing going on the entire weekend. This was during the height of the COVID-19 shutdown, so even Sunday morning church was online. I was looking at spending the next seventy hours by myself at home.

I made it through Friday evening and went to bed. When Saturday morning came, I found myself in a panic at this thought of being alone all weekend. I can only describe it as a feeling similar to claustrophobia. It literally felt as if the walls of the house were coming closer together, and I had to get out.

I picked up my phone, started in the *A*'s, and began texting friends.

"Hey, what are you up to?" I would ask. "I am in serious need of getting out of the house. Do you have anything going on tonight?"

If this text sounds desperate, it is because it was. The first one to respond with an open schedule was my buddy, Allen. Allen and I had grown up together but hadn't spent much time together in our adult lives. We decided to meet at Jack Stack Barbeque in Kansas City. Before the night was over, we were sitting around the campfire in the backyard of another mutual friend, Matt. It soon dawned on me that each of the three of us were currently facing the most difficult battle in our lives. I desperately needed them in my life at that moment, but each of them also needed me.

The beginning of loneliness

Loneliness is very prevalent during a separation. However, it should be noted for many, loneliness begins well before the marriage ends. Marriages don't fall apart and end overnight. Granted, they may end quickly when a deep, dark secret is brought to life, such as an affair. For most, the internal separation begins long before the physical separation takes place. For some, great loneliness takes place even though your spouse may be sleeping next to you. However, even though they are there in body, there can be a great emotional distance between you. That is possibly the most difficult type of loneliness to face: the kind where you are so close in proximity but yet are worlds apart.

You may have come out of a relationship with a broken person. There are so many broken people in this world looking to other people to fill the voids within them. "Broken people break other people," remarked Alissa, "and they cannot have healthy relationships." You may have gone into your marriage as a fairly healthy person, and now you find yourself broken by the one who promised to "love and cherish" you. Now, *you* are broken and trying to piece your life back together.

One other truth to realize and acknowledge is understanding that each of us feels hurt and lonely because part of our heart is still shared with the person who is now gone. When we said "I do," we began our lives together. The journey of marriage may have lasted one year or fifty years, but during the marriage we faced mutual obstacles, lived through mutual experiences, made mutual friends, and shared our most intimate struggles, successes, and moments together. Regardless of what caused the separation to take place, each of those shared memories will continue to play out in our minds. Two hearts became one, and the separating of those hearts is an agonizing process. The separation causes a hole in your heart, and that hole will need time and TLC to heal. Refusing to acknowledge its existence will only delay the healing process.

Loneliness versus being alone

Sometimes, it is easy to confuse loneliness with being alone. A person going through a divorce will often think, *If I can just finalize this divorce and find someone else, I will be happy again.* However, they are confusing their hurt with loneliness. Their heart has been ripped to shreds, but in their mind, getting a new person will fill the hole left by the agonizing process of separation and divorce. Is it any wonder that 67 percent of second marriages and 74 percent of third marriages again end in divorce?[17]

When attempting to fill that hole in your heart with another person before you have healed, you are allowing yourself to go into a new relationship as a broken person. The relationship is already unhealthy because you are unhealthy. You are trying to use the other person to cover your hurts and heal your wounds rather than allowing time, counseling, and God to heal you and make you whole again.

---

[17] https://divorcestrategiesgroup.com/why-second-marriages-fail

The truth is this: loneliness begins internally; therefore, external fixes will only act as a Band-Aid. Tami remembers, "Some of the worst loneliness was not when I was by myself, but when I would go to events like the Christmas program. I'm sitting there by myself and everyone else has a spouse, and there I am (alone)." Alissa recalls a similar feeling. "I have been surrounded by people, had my child on my lap, with people I love all over the room, and my heart aches because of loneliness. It's an intimacy I miss."

Jesus knows

In chapter 4, we found Jesus in the Garden of Gethsemane emotionally exhausted while He prayed. Let's revisit that scene. In Luke 22:41–46, we read:

> He walked away, about a stone's throw, and knelt down and prayed, "Father, if you are willing, please take this cup of suffering away from me. Yet I want your will to be done, not mine."
>
> Then an angel from heaven appeared and strengthened Him. He prayed more fervently, and He was in such agony of spirit that His sweat fell to the ground like great drops of blood. At last, He stood up again and returned to the disciples, only to find them asleep, exhausted from grief.
>
> "Why are you sleeping?" He asked them. "Get up and pray, so that you will not give in to temptation."

One thing surprising to me after I was married was how much I still lived so much of my life alone. While this was sometimes true in relation to physical proximity, it was even truer mentally. Inside my head, I still made plans, thought through things, debated what to say and do, and so on. I now had another person close by whom I needed to discuss things with, but I still lived my own separate life within my head.

Here we seem to see this same idea playing out with Jesus. He and his disciples go to the Garden of Gethsemane. The disciples are distressed at this point because of the other events which took place that evening with Judas, but they have not grasped the full scope of what Jesus is facing. Jesus walks away a "stone's throw" and begins praying a fervent, agonizing prayer, causing Him to sweat blood. This is the darkest night of Jesus's life, but when He walks back to the disciples, they are sleeping. Jesus is facing tremendous inner turmoil, and yet those closest to Him seem to be somewhat oblivious and unconcerned. Jesus must have felt so alone.

Later in Luke 22, we see the story of Peter denying Jesus three times. This takes place only a few hours after Jesus's desperate and lonely prayer in the garden. Beginning with verse 60, we read:

> But Peter said, "Man, I don't know what you are talking about."
>
> And immediately, while he was still speaking, the rooster crowed. At that moment, the Lord turned and looked at Peter.
>
> Suddenly, the Lord's words flashed through Peter's mind: "Before the rooster crows tomorrow morning, you will deny three times that you even know me."
>
> And Peter left the courtyard, weeping bitterly. The guards in charge of Jesus began mocking and beating Him.
>
> They blindfolded Him and said, "Prophesy to us! Who hit you that time?" And they hurled all sorts of terrible insults at Him.

Jesus and Peter exchanged one last look as Peter turns and leaves, "weeping bitterly." Jesus's friends and followers have now forsaken Him as He is mocked, beaten, blindfolded, and insulted. Jesus was not alone. No, there were people all around Him, but the loneliness He must have felt at that moment is greater than any of us will ever face. Jesus knew what it was like to feel intense loneliness.

My story, continued

As I sat in my friend's backyard that night, I began to see even more clearly the importance of surrounding myself with good friends. We laughed together, came close to crying together, and renewed our friendships. It has been more than two years since that night, but we have continued to strengthen each other with conversations, texts, prayers, and support. That night began the rekindling of old friendships and was a turning point in my healing journey. However, none of it would have happened if I wouldn't have picked up the phone and began reaching out in a desperate attempt to combat my loneliness.

While the struggles you face are internal, the burdens can be greatly reduced when you surround yourself with close friends and family who are willing to help you in your walk through the valley. However, most people do not know what to do or how to help, and this may only come after you let them know they are wanted and needed. While this takes vulnerability on your part and commitment on their part, you will both be rewarded. After all, Galatians 6:2 says, "Bear ye one another's burdens, and so fulfil the law of Christ." It is a privilege to walk alongside a friend in need. However, that hole in your heart and the loneliness you feel can only be totally healed by the one that died to bring you "life more abundant."[18]

Alissa's story

Late one night, Alissa found herself driving the back roads as she cried and prayed. This had become somewhat of a routine as Alissa used the car and driving as her way to clear her head. This particular night, as she drove, she found herself weeping as she cried out to God.

"God," she prayed, "please just let someone call and check on me. Wake them up. Please, I'm so lonely. Why don't you care?"

---

[18] John 10:10

At that moment, she recalled the still small voice of the Holy Spirit saying, "I'm right here."

"But you're not a person. You're not talking to me. I can't audibly hear your voice. I want to talk on the phone to someone."

Then Alissa felt the Holy Spirit respond, "Why am I not enough for you?"

In that moment, Alissa was both convicted and hurt.

"God, you are enough," she responded, "but you're not in my car. You are not on my phone. I can't hear your voice."

Again, the Spirit responded, "What are we doing right now?"

"It wrecked me," Alissa said, "because I began to realize He has always been there and was always there." Alissa began to praise God because "if others were calling, I wouldn't be talking to You," she told God.

Alissa began to see "this journey was not just about me, it's about many people, and it's about my story, and it's about me finding Him in my pain, and realizing He is enough."

Conclusion

Loneliness is so very real, and it is so very painful. In order to remedy it, you must begin internally. Your heart has been ripped apart. A Band-Aid will not fix a hole in your heart. Find those close friends and family that you trust and ask them to walk with you and help strengthen you during this difficult season in life. Most of all, you must throw yourself into the unfailing and all-powerful arms of your Creator. He made you, and only He can fix and fill that void within you. Call out to Jesus because "He is enough."

Psalm 23 (Complete Jewish Bible): A psalm of David

> ADONAI is my shepherd; I lack nothing.
> He has me lie down in grassy pastures, He leads me by quiet water,
> He restores my inner person. He guides me in right paths for the sake of His own name.

Even if I pass through death-dark ravines, I will fear no disaster; for You are with me;

your rod and staff reassure me.

You prepare a table for me, even as my enemies watch;

You anoint my head with oil from an overflowing cup.

Goodness and grace will pursue me every day of my life;

and I will live in the house of *Adonai* for years and years to come.

Chapter 7

Should I Have Done More

> I wasn't realizing that he needed more of me than I was giving him. I probably wasn't as attentive as I should have been.
>
> —Beth

> Your heart can only take so much pain.
>
> —Susan

> *I am leaving you with a gift—peace of mind and heart. And the peace I give is a gift the world cannot give. So don't be troubled or afraid.*
>
> —John 14:27 NLT

Tami's story

Tami had married young, and like many young couples, her marriage quickly turned into one argument after another. This wasn't how she thought it would be. Even though Tami had made a commitment to her marriage and had a beautiful five-year-old, she was tired of trying. "I was extremely selfish, and I just wanted out," Tami recalled. "I even had another divorced mom come to me and say, 'Please think about what you are doing. It's harder than you realize.'" No amount of pleading was going to change Tami's mind. "I was determined to get out. I did not think about anything. I gave up everything. I didn't take anything. I just left."

After a few years, Tami remarried. Her second marriage was worse than the first. Tami eventually found herself in the middle of an abusive marriage. For years, she took the abuse while trying to diffuse situations and apologizing for even the smallest things in order to appease her husband. This time, however, Tami was determined to make it work. The day finally came when Tami's husband walked out on her and their children. Her second marriage had ended.

Today, after many years have passed, Tami looks back on both failed marriages. Ironically, Tami felt very little regret when she walked out on her first marriage. "Years later, I thought, I should have just done what was right and stayed, and maybe we would have gotten old enough to figure something out," she said. However, her mindset was totally different in her second marriage. This time, she questioned many parts of her marriage and had "a thousand and one 'should haves.'" *I should have been a better person. I should have tried harder. I should have done more, and if I could have, maybe he wouldn't have left*, Tami thought.

Tami tried to get her husband to stay and, after he left, tried to get him to come back. She was willing to say or do almost anything to make the marriage work. Why? Why would Tami seemingly so flippantly walk out on her first marriage but be willing to endure abuse and become "a nothing with no personality" but yet feel like her "world had fallen apart" when her second marriage ended?

Questions

After the breaking apart of any marriage, there is going to be a time of questioning oneself. "Should I have done more? What should I have done differently? Did I cause this to happen? Could I have prevented this from happening?" If you have not asked yourself those questions, I believe, one of three things is happening: (1) Your separation may still be so fresh and your mind occupied with a thousand other thoughts that you have not yet stopped to look at yourself and inside yourself for answers. (2) You are too busy blaming your spouse and casting them in a bad light to look at the part you played in the breakup. (3) You already know what the answers will be, so you refuse to ask yourself the questions.

Before you close this book and throw it into the fire, please let me finish. I am convinced that very few marriages end because each spouse was 50 percent at fault. It may be a 60/40 percent split or a 90/10 percent split or even 99/1 percent, but only in the rarest of cases would one person be responsible for 100 percent of the blame. Therefore, what could or should I have done differently?

When you honestly ask yourself the questions, you are accomplishing two things. First, closure will only come when you go through the difficult process of walking through the pain and seeking honest answers. Please keep in mind some answers will never come but others will. Also, realize that the answers may hurt. We all generally consider ourselves to be good people. We seek the approval of others and want them to view us as kind, thoughtful, and caring people. When I look deep within and realize I spoke a word in anger and frustration which cannot be taken back, it hurts. When I see I intentionally or unintentionally did something that brought heartache to the one I vowed to love, my heart begins to ache as well. When I realize I did not give the proper worth to someone else, I begin to feel the pain I caused. My body language, words, actions, and even my reactions have consequences. I must be willing to be honest with myself about what I have done.

When looking back at what could have been done differently, Beth remarked, "I think I would figure out a better way to solve the communication problems." Don stated, "I think I would have tried to have more conversations one-on-one with her." Mark stated, "Maybe I would have pushed harder to go to counseling." Only by asking questions can we come up with answers.

"So why does it matter?" you may ask. "The marriage is over." True, but there is a second task you can accomplish by honestly asking yourself the tough questions. When you sincerely discover your part in the weakening of the marriage, you have taken the first step in preventing it from happening again in a potential future marriage relationship or in other relationships in general. Many first marriages fall apart, turning into second and third marriages which again fall apart because we are not honest with ourselves about our part in the breakdown of the relationship. Whether you are responsible for 1 percent or 99 percent, you must work to fix what you are able to in order for relationships to be successful down the road.

Tami's story continues

So what causes someone like Tami to walk out on a marriage with some problems but yet stay at all costs when he or she is being abused? For Tami, some of it stemmed from her upbringing. Tami believed divorce was wrong, and now she found herself on the brink of a second failed marriage. Today, many people find themselves divorced, but the thought of being divorced a second time brought great "shame" to Tami.

The second reason Tami clung so tightly to her second marriage was possibly due to some form of "trauma bonding." The kind of trauma bonding most of us are familiar with is "Stockholm syndrome." This is where a captive begins to develop feelings of sympathy for their captor. However, trauma bonding can take place in child-parent relationships where a parent is abusive to a child, and in the child's mind, abuse becomes connected with love. It is also very common in domestic relationships where one spouse is abusive, followed by a time of perceived sorrow and regret, possible romance and gifting, only to be repeated again. It is a never-ending cycle. Trauma bonding is a psychological response to abuse. It occurs when the abused person forms an unhealthy bond with the person who abuses them.[19]

Please understand I am not an expert on "trauma bonding" nor do I have the ability to diagnose such a condition in anyone. However, abuse causes the brain to be warped, and our thoughts can quickly become warped as well. "You have to understand the whole abuse mentality," Tami says. She used to reason, "Obviously it was my fault that he hit me. I should have been a better person. I should

---

[19] https://www.medicalnewstoday.com/articles/trauma-bonding

have tried harder. I should have done more, and if I could have, then maybe he wouldn't have left." When you step back and look at such a response from the outside, you can easily see the fallacy in such reasoning, however, when you are in the midst of such a situation, the mind can easily present thoughts and ideas to you that seem reasonable, even though they are blatantly false.

Alissa's story

Alissa knows full well the pain of being in an abusive relationship. For years, she suffered all kinds of abuse. Her situation became so bad that her own very conservative family began telling her it was time to get out. Her family was worried about her mental health and even her physical safety. "I'm as stubborn as a mule," Alissa said, and she refused to leave the marriage until she had done "everything" she could possibly do to "fix" it. It got to the point that some of those closest to Alissa began distancing themselves from her.

Today, Alissa can tell you the date when God "freed" her from her marriage and told her it was time to "get out." "There was absolutely no earthly or heavenly thing I could have done at that point," Alissa said. "If you stay in it until God releases you, your outcome brings peace, which I would have been robbed of, had I done what the people in my life wanted me to do when they wanted me to do it in their time frame instead of God's."

Alissa continued, "God gave me peace, and God gave me freedom. Because I waited until He gave me that peace and that freedom. Even right now it makes me feel amazing He did that. You move when God tells you to move." Today, Alissa doesn't struggle with the question of "Should I have done more?" because she is confident that the answer is "No."

Conclusion

In this chapter, we waded deep into the subject of abusive marriages. I want to note that, while the stories told were both about women being abused, abuse can go either way. While men are usually not physically abused, it does happen. Also, verbal abuse from a spouse can certainly happen to either a husband or a wife. The effects of any kind of abuse can last long after the marriage is over. The depth of those effects is greater the longer it is allowed to continue. If you are the victim of an abusive marriage of any kind, please seek professional help and counseling. Your brain has been damaged because of the abuse, and only through the help of God and those professionally trained to help can you begin to retrain your brain to be whole again.

If you have begun to ask yourself the hard questions and have discovered some difficult answers, you must now begin to reconcile and heal. If you have a civil relationship with your former spouse, you may want to write or tell them you are sorry for those specific things that you did that led to the decay of your marriage. Most of all, pray and ask God to forgive you for the things you did wrong. Once you do this, learn from your mistakes and move on.

As you walk through the valley of divorce, some of the graves you see will be there because of you. In front of you lies an empty grave. Toss all these questions and answers in that empty hole, reconcile where possible, and cover it up with God's forgiveness. On the tombstone, fill in after the dash the date you have done all you can. Those questions and regrets are now buried. Leave them there; it's time to move on down the path.

Psalm 23 (Christian Standard Bible): The Good Shepherd, A psalm of David

> The LORD is my shepherd; I have what I need.
> He lets me lie down in green pastures; He leads me beside quiet waters.
> He renews my life; He leads me along the right paths for His name's sake.
> Even when I go through the darkest valley, I fear no danger, for You are with me; your rod and your staff—they comfort me.

You prepare a table before me in the presence of my enemies; You anoint my head with oil; my cup overflows.

Only goodness and faithful love will pursue me all the days of my life, and I will dwell in the house of the Lord as long as I live.

Chapter 8

Worse than Death

Nobody brings you a casserole
when you get a divorce.

—Susan

They both are very tough at the
time, for different reasons.

—Beth

*The Lord is close to the brokenhearted; He
rescues those whose spirits are crushed.*

—*Psalm 34:18 NLT*

Beth's story

Beth had been divorced for over sixteen years. Even though a great amount of time had passed, Beth still struggled with internal issues of shame, worry, and wondering about God's forgiveness. Would God even forgive her for getting divorced? "I now had the title of 'divorcee,' a title that I wouldn't ideally look for in a mate. Yet I wanted someone who would accept and love me despite the label," Beth recalled. "I didn't know if it was right for me to look for somebody. I just thought that if it was meant to be, that God would send somebody my way."

Beth's son grew up and headed off to college. For the first time in her adult life, Beth found herself truly alone. Four months after her son went away, Beth went to a fundraiser at a local Christian college where she ran into an old acquaintance named David. Beth and David enjoyed lunch together which sparked an interest in both of them, soon leading to a dating relationship. This new love proved to be the knight in shining armor that Beth had been seeking for so long. All her fear that she had about letting another man in her life soon melted away, and it wasn't long before Beth again found herself at the altar saying, "I do."

Soon into the marriage, Beth knew that she had found the man she had longed for. Not only did David treat her right, but he also helped her through some of her struggles as she began to come to terms with and find peace from the memories, doubts, and fears that had hounded her since her divorce. This is how marriage was meant to be.

Seven months after David and Beth were married, they received devastating news that David's cancer had returned. The man she had leaned on for her healing now found himself in need of a physical healing. The following three-and-a-half years were a roller coaster for Beth and David. One day would bring a good report and hope while the next day might bring just the opposite. In the end, with Beth by his side, David lost his battle with cancer, and Beth lost her best friend.

Their four-year marriage was over not because either of them wished for it to end, but rather because death had forced this happy couple to say goodbye long before either of them ever wanted to utter the words. For a second time, Beth found herself single and alone.

Worse than death

It has been said that divorce is worse than death. Is that the case however? If you find yourself right now immersed in the valley of divorce, living each day and moment with the pain of rejection, shame, and betrayal so ever-present, you might yell out a resounding "Yes! This is worse than any other emotional pain a human can endure." However, if you have stood by the bedside of your spouse as they breathed their last breath or been blindsided by the news that your spouse was killed in an accident, you might yell out, "No! Nothing is worse than this pain and devastation that I feel right now." The answer is not a simple one, and we must look deeper to truly understand.

Author Sonyan White states that "death and divorce loss share the seven stages of grief." These stages are 1. Denial, 2. Pain and Fear, 3. Anger, 4. Bargaining, 5. Guilt, 6. Depression, and 7. Acceptance.[20] For those who have not experienced the loss of a spouse to divorce or death, some of these stages might not seem to make sense. For those who have experienced them, each action or emotion has been felt strongly at one time or another.

Similarities between death and divorce

Whether you lost your spouse to death or to divorce, there are some similarities you will find on either path you must travel. Beth recalls, "You are lonely in both. This is a couples' world we live in. In either case, you are by yourself. You have lost dreams. Your future is uncertain. There is a loss of extended family. That's hard. There are financial concerns. Basically, you lose your person."

The difficult path that Beth has traveled, experiencing the loss of a spouse to both death and divorce, is a path that others have also traveled. Terry knows the pain of both paths as well. When I asked Terry to compare her experiences, she responded, "In both cases, divorce and death, it is an adjustment transitioning from being a couple to being single. For example, couples don't usually invite you out anymore, so your social life tends to revolve around singles. However, I felt like the adjustment was easier in the case of divorce because the extremely painful marriage made singleness a relief."

Looking back to the seven stages of grief, one may notice "anger" on the list and wonder how this would relate to a person who lost his or her spouse to death. Obviously, there could be anger directed toward God or the situation that caused the death, but surely, the grieving spouse would not be angry toward their loving spouse who had died, right?

---

[20] https://www.sonyanwhitecoaching.com/how-death-and-divorce-compare

One evening, I sat down with a friend of mine named Kelly and asked for her thoughts on this subject. Kelly has not felt the sting of divorce like everyone else I interviewed, but Kelly is very familiar with the devastation of death. In November of 2019, Kelly lost her husband Travis in a car accident. In an instant, Kelly's world came crashing down upon her. Her life was changed forever.

As we sat and talked that night, Kelly tried for twenty minutes to put her thoughts into words. For a week leading up to our meeting, Kelly pondered this question but attempting to quantify the severity of the pain of one versus the other while her heart still hurt from losing her husband was a task too difficult. "I feel almost like I'm just mad at him for leaving," Kelly said of the man she had loved her entire adult life, "and for all the things that I now had to think about, that I just wish he would have helped me before he left." She continued, "I had some days when I just felt mad that he was gone." Was Kelly truly mad at her husband? No. Kelly was undergoing the grieving process.

Then Kelly truly put into words the reason for all the pain and emotion. "*Our depth of grief is because of our depth of love.*" That's it. The vast range of these emotions that we face in either a death or a divorce all stem from our choice to love. All the way back in chapter 1, we talked about rejection and how those closest to us—whether a friend, family member, or spouse—have the ability to inflict the most pain on us because of our love for them. When your spouse dies, it hurts. Why? Because of your depth of love for them. When your spouse leaves, it hurts. Why? Because of the love you have or had for them. When we open ourselves up to love deeply, we open ourselves up to be hurt deeply as well. Then Kelly said, "No matter the situation, when it's *your* situation, it hurts." We can all relate to that.

Jesus wept

In John 11, we find the story of Jesus raising Lazarus from the dead. While Lazarus was on his deathbed in Bethany, his sisters, Mary and Martha, sent word to Jesus that Lazarus was very ill. In verse 5, we read: "Now Jesus loved Martha and her sister and Lazarus" (NIV).

However, it was a few days later when Jesus finally arrived, only to discover that Lazarus had been dead for four days.

As Jesus came near, we see Mary go out to meet Jesus in verse 32:

> When Mary reached the place where Jesus was and saw him, she fell at his feet and said, "Lord, if you had been here, my brother would not have died."
> When Jesus saw her weeping, and the Jews who had come along with her also weeping, He was deeply moved in spirit and troubled.
> "Where have you laid him?" He asked.
> "Come and see, Lord," they replied.

This says that Jesus was "deeply moved in spirit and troubled." Other translations say Jesus was angered. In the next verse, however, we see two words that seem puzzling at first. It simply says, "Jesus wept." Jesus wept? Did Jesus weep because Lazarus was dead? I don't think so. After all, Jesus told Martha back in verse 23, "your brother will rise again." Jesus had made this journey knowing full well that he would raise Lazarus back to life. So why did Jesus weep?

We find our answer way back in verse 5. Jesus wept not because Lazarus was dead. That was temporary. He wept because of the depth of His love for Mary, Martha, and Lazarus. Jesus was showing His humanity, and the depth of *His* grief was directly related to the depth of *their* grief and the love and sympathy that He felt toward them.

Just as Jesus grieved for Mary, Martha, and Lazarus because of His love toward them, you and I will grieve at the loss of our spouse. This loss is felt whether a spouse chooses to leave or is taken from us by death. "Our depth of grief is because of our depth of love."

Differences between death and divorce

Please don't misunderstand what I am attempting to say. When a spouse chooses to leave or chooses to give their love to someone else, many strong emotions are going to begin to well up within you. You will feel anger because of rejection, you will feel bitterness because of betrayal, and you will possibly feel hatred because of hurt; however, none of these feelings would reach the level they do if you had been rejected, betrayed, and hurt by someone that you cared little about. *We often try to mask how much we cared in order to attempt to minimize how much we hurt.* However, you must understand and acknowledge the source of your pain before you can begin to effectively treat it.

While the source may be the same, the situation is definitely different. "With a divorce, you have lost a bad thing," stated Beth, but "with a death, you have lost a good thing." I should acknowledge that, many times, divorce not only results in the loss of a spouse but also in the loss of children. We will look at this aspect in Section 4 of this book, "The Children of Divorce."

Susan related something her Sunday school teacher had told her when Susan was going through her divorce. "Nobody brings you a casserole when you get a divorce," the teacher said, "but when you lose someone [to death], the lasagnas and the casseroles start piling in." Susan continued, "It's like this big silence comes and the silence doesn't come with flowers for the casket. It doesn't come with money for the funeral expenses. Divorce is this large void that people don't know how to fill."

Along with divorce come some of the aforementioned feelings and emotions that are not present with death. "The separation that takes place in death is just as permanent, but it's not something that is done by choice. So maybe the grief is for a different reason," Don commented. "When it's a divorce, there has been a betrayal, so theoretically, it might be more painful because of that sense of rejection that you feel." Tami had a similar thought, "I've only lost a mom as far as anybody real close to me, and she didn't have a choice to leave me. She was sick. I was sad and brokenhearted, but I didn't feel rejection. With the divorce, I just feel like that hit me harder because the choice was made to leave me, which implies all kinds of things like 'you're not good enough' and so on."

Beth recalled, "When a spouse dies, you first think about all the stuff [circumstances] at the end [surrounding the death]. You think about all the bad stuff. That does fade. Then the good stuff [memories] comes out more. With the divorce, I had a hard time for years—thinking back, reflecting back, and figuring out what was real. Was the good stuff really good? How stupid was I? What was real?" She continued, "Going through my divorce, I had a really hard time sleeping. I would lay in bed, and I didn't want to think about the present because it was just crazy. I couldn't think about the past because I didn't know what was real, and I didn't want to think about the future because I couldn't imagine it. I couldn't figure out what to think about in order to go to sleep at night."

The finality of death versus the fragility of divorce

While a small percentage (10 to 15 percent) of divorced couples eventually get back together,[21] losing a spouse to death is final. This finality is extremely difficult, but is it worse than the fragility of divorce? Terry, after losing a spouse to death and then one to divorce, sees the finality of death in a positive light. "I definitely think that divorce is harder than death. For one thing, death is final," Terry remarked. "That part of your life is over, and you learn how to move on to a new normal. If your husband was a Christian, you know that he is in a far better place! On the other hand, a true end of a relationship in a divorce is often much messier and not as clear. There are often lingering issues that make communication and feelings continue between the two people. This might make it harder for people to move on in their lives."

Mark has a similar thought, "I think divorce is worse than losing a spouse to death because that other person is still around. There are those times when you see that person and it brings everything back, and that's difficult. In death, it's over. It's done. And yes, it's painful, but there is, if not closure, a finality. With divorce, that finality never happens. Other than that piece of paper that you put in your strongbox, there is no finality."

For Alissa, an abuse survivor, this thought was magnified. "For me," she said, "the divorce part that is harder than death is that they

---

[21] https://www.jonnyklaw.com/blog/2020/february

are still alive. You can still run into them… I would have preferred death over divorce because divorce means that no matter how much I heal, at any point, there can be pressure in the ripping back of those scabs that are over the healing and the pushing on that wound. When someone is gone, they are gone, and it leaves a void. But at least there is not a fear of them resurfacing. When you are divorced, at any moment you can turn around, and they can be there."

Kelly, who experienced the finality of death, looks at the question through a different lens. "Even if I was furious at him, I would still be glad that he was on earth. That he was around." Kelly, now left to care for their three teenaged girls, also looks at it through the eyes of their daughters. "I think that, for the girls' sake, for big decisions concerning the girls, I think the option of him still being around would be beneficial for the girls. But I also don't know how it would be devastating to my girls in other ways." As she continued to ponder the question, Kelly stated, "Maybe if he had left us, maybe there would be a point where I could just move on… I really, really, really don't like being sad. I think there would be times when it would just be easier to be mad." Again, anger exists in both situations; however, it is much easier to direct that anger when a spouse leaves versus when a spouse is taken away.

David mourns the death of Absalom

In chapters 1 to 3 of this book, we looked at the story of King David and the rejection and betrayal from his son Absalom. As we close out section 2, let's again take a look at this story of David and Absalom.

After a long journey, David and his men arrived at Mahanaim. While there, they regrouped and refreshed. King David knew that Absalom and his men would soon come and attempt to destroy David and his army once and for all. The day soon came when word reached David that Absalom and his army were coming. As David's army prepared to go out and meet them, David told his generals, "Joab, Abishai, and Ittai: 'For my sake, deal gently with young

Absalom.' And all the troops heard the king give this order to his commanders."[22]

The battle raged on, and more than twenty thousand men died that day. Absalom came upon some of David's men and attempted to escape. However, as he rode, his hair got entangled in some low branches, and Absalom found himself hanging helplessly by his hair from the branch. When Joab saw Absalom in this helpless position, he drove three daggers into the heart of David's son. Absalom died, and the army of David was victorious.[23]

Meanwhile, David waited restlessly for news of the battle to arrive. We pick up the story in verse 31.

> Then the man from Ethiopia arrived and said, "I have good news for my lord the king. Today, the LORD has rescued you from all those who rebelled against you."
>
> "What about young Absalom?" the king demanded. "Is he all right?"
>
> And the Ethiopian replied, "May all of your enemies, my lord the king, both now and in the future, share the fate of that young man!"
>
> The king was overcome with emotion. He went up to the room over the gateway and burst into tears.
>
> And as he went, he cried, "O my son Absalom! My son, my son Absalom! If only I had died instead of you! O Absalom, my son, my son."

Three chapters earlier in 2 Samuel 15:30, we had seen David weeping as he walked up the Mount of Olives with his head covered and his feet bare as a sign of mourning. That time, David had felt the powerful sting of rejection from his son. Now we again see David weeping as he "was overcome with emotion" at the death of his son.

---

[22] 2 Samuel 18:5
[23] 2 Samuel 18:7–15

Grant it, Absalom was David's son, but he was also David's enemy and his greatest threat to survival. With the death of Absalom, David's exile would be over, and David would, in all likelihood, return home and take his rightful place back on the throne as the king of Israel. This was a great victory for David and his men, yet David cared little about the victory because he was mourning the loss of his son Absalom. David lamented this loss as he cried, "If only I had died instead of you."

Acceptance

Like David, the sudden loss of a close family member or spouse is going to be met with great mourning. In an instant, your life is changed forever. You were not allowed to prepare for it, and now you must give up your dreams, hopes, plans, and most of all, your partner for a new way of life that looks so ominous. What happens, however, when you do have a chance to get your affairs in order or plan for the departure of a spouse due to death or divorce?

Sonyan White addresses this when she writes comparing death and divorce. "Many people are blindsided by their divorce and your spouse's abrupt decision to leave the marriage can be just as shocking and traumatic as a sudden death. Many people feel that divorce is even worse than death when rejection, betrayal, and shame are added to the loss.

"In other cases, the breakdown of a marriage happens over a long period of time, and the ongoing pain and fear of the inevitable is comparable to a spouse slowly dying of a terminal illness. In these situations, a divorce or death can be a welcome relief from the prolonged pain and suffering."[24]

Terry spoke of this acceptance when she said, "Because Tom and I both had such faith and trust in God, it was not hard for me to accept that Tom's death was God's will, or at least in God's plan." Her acceptance was not as easy after her divorce. "Since I know that divorce is not God's first plan for a couple, it took me a long time to

---

[24] https://www.sonyanwhitecoaching.com/how-death-and-divorce-compare

come to terms with the reality that separation was the only option left. Again, accepting divorce was certainly harder than accepting death."

The final answer

So is divorce worse than death? For several pages, we have looked at how each one is difficult in its own way. Which one is worse? I think the answer is clear. Simply put, it depends. That's right. It depends. There is no cookie-cutter answer that covers all situations. Is the death sudden or after a long illness? Did the divorce come as a shock due to an affair or some other unforeseen sin, or did it come as a welcome relief after the pain of rejection, dishonesty, abuse, or any number of other factors? Are there children involved? There are so many variables that must be factored in to come up with the answer. Each situation is different, but every situation brings about great pain and grief.

Each divorce carries with it a stigma which doesn't exist with a death. However, the reaction of many outside your inner circle will be very similar in both cases. We will discuss this in Section 3, "The Church." This one thing I know, just as Jesus wept when He saw the tears of Mary and Martha, He also weeps with us whether our pain is caused by death or by divorce. He is familiar with stigma, and He is affected by death. He has experienced rejection, grief, sorrow, and affliction. He weeps with us because He has felt our hurt. The Prophet Isaiah put this into words when he wrote Isaiah 53:3–5:

> He is despised and rejected by men,
> A man of sorrows and acquainted with grief.
> And we hid, as it were, *our* faces from Him;
> He was despised, and we did not esteem Him.
> Surely He has borne our griefs
> And carried our sorrows;
> Yet we esteemed Him stricken,
> Smitten by God, and afflicted.
> But He *was* wounded for our transgressions,

> *He was* bruised for our iniquities;
> The chastisement for our peace *was* upon Him,
> And by His stripes we are healed. (NKJV)

Does Jesus care? Oh, yes, He cares! Whether your path through the valley is due to the death of a spouse or due to the death of a marriage, you do not walk the path alone. The path is easy to follow because Jesus has blazed a trail. He understands every pain. He has felt every hurt. He has been despised and rejected by man, but yet He continues to love each and every one of us. Follow in His footsteps. It will lead you out of the valley and back to stable ground.

Psalm 23 (Amplified Bible): The Lord, the Psalmist's Shepherd, A psalm of David

> The Lord is my Shepherd [to feed, to guide, and to shield me], I shall not want.
>
> He lets me lie down in green pastures; He leads me beside the still *and* quiet waters.
>
> He refreshes *and* restores my soul (life); He leads me in the paths of righteousness for His name's sake.
>
> Even though I walk through the [sunless] valley of the shadow of death, I fear no evil, for You are with me; Your rod [to protect] and Your staff [to guide], they comfort *and* console me.
>
> You prepare a table before me in the presence of my enemies.
>
> You have anointed *and* refreshed my head with oil; my cup overflows.
>
> Surely goodness and mercy *and* unfailing love shall follow me all the days of my life, and I shall dwell forever [throughout all my days] in the house *and* in the presence of the Lord.

SECTION 3

The Church

There is a reason God hates divorce. I think it has to do with the fact that His children are ripped apart and left destroyed, so He hates that. That's a god of love. That's not a god of justice. A god that's crying because you're crying because you're ripped apart. He hates divorce because it rips people apart and hurts them.

—Tami

The LORD is my rock, my fortress, and my savior.
My God is my rock, in whom I find protection.
He is my shield, the power that saves me,
and my place of safety.

—Psalm 18:2

The church

No one sets out to become a statistic. You were no different. At the beginning, you knew that you would have a strong marriage. It would be the kind of marriage that others would look to with envy. Perhaps you had parents that modeled a great marriage in front of you daily. It didn't really look that difficult. You were determined, committed, and in love. Your marriage was going to be wonderful.

Now you sit in an empty house with a thousand thoughts running through your head. How did you become a statistic? How would this change your life? How would people view you now that you are separated from your spouse? Then a thought blindsides you like a right hook from a heavyweight boxer that you never saw coming. What about my church?

What are all those people in your church going to think about you, and how are they going to view you? Not your closest friends—you have been talking to them about your marriage difficulties for quite some time. But the rest of the church has only viewed you through the lens that you provided them to look through. Even in your most difficult times at home, you could always manage to go to church, put on your Sunday mask, and act as if everything were perfect as you smiled and greeted your church family.

Now that lens was going to be ripped from their vision like a cataract surgically removed, thus pulling back the veil and bringing into focus your true world that really exists. Your church family is now going to have a firsthand look at your failed marriage. How will they react? Will you be deemed unfit to teach that Sunday school class or kids' church that you have taught for so long? Will anyone respect you enough to come to your Bible study? Did your opportunity for ministry just die along with your marriage?

What will happen when you walk through those doors on Sunday morning? You are so desperately in need of help and support. The question is, will you find it at your church?

Chapter 9

How Did I Become a Statistic?

> Now I had children that would go to VBS, and people would say, "They have two different last names and neither of them is their mom's." That wasn't supposed to be from a Christian home. That wasn't supposed to happen.
>
> —Tami

> I can remember, as I was younger, hearing things that were said about divorced people and thinking less of individuals who were divorced. Then I find myself, years later of course, in the same situation. That was kind of difficult.
>
> —Mark

> *The LORD is good, a strong refuge when trouble comes. He is close to those who trust in Him.*
>
> —*Nahum 1:7 NLT*

Our stories

I suppose that everyone, whether they grew up in a Christian home or not, feels some degree of stigma when they get divorced. After all, no one wants to admit that they failed at something. However, that stigma is worse when you grew up in a stable, two-parent Christian home, found the love of your life, got married, and then felt the pain and shame of your marriage falling apart.

The seven main characters of this book, myself included, all have two things in common. First, we have all walked through this dark valley of divorce. Second, each of us grew up in a stable, Christian home. Our parents loved us and loved each other. For most of us, marriage success stories can be traced back from one generation to the next. Our grandparents and even our great-grandparents were able to navigate the ups and downs of life and stuck together through it all.

Growing up in this environment with those examples before us is a great blessing. I would not ever wish to have a different heritage than that. However, when that is your heritage, being the one to break this positive, successful cycle brings about a great stigma. Not only am I now in the 40 percent that are divorced, but I am on the opposite side of the spectrum than my parents, grandparents, great-grandparents, and so on, who are in the 60 percent of couples that stayed together.

This stigma is exacerbated when you bring the church into the mix. We all grew up hearing sermons about the evils of divorce and how God hates divorce. It is true that God hates divorce. Any loving god would not want to see his children torn apart emotionally and mentally by such a devastating thing as divorce. A loving god would never seek to see children forced to watch their parents split up, leaving them to question what part they had in the demise of the marriage as they now struggle with feelings of insecurity, doubt, and despair. God does hate divorce, but God unconditionally loves those who bear the dreaded *D* figuratively upon their chest.

In many cases, our minds were conditioned, probably unintentionally, to look down on someone who is divorced. Now, like an ironic twist of fate in a horror movie, we find ourselves in a position we never would have imagined, wondering if the church that taught us to hate divorce will still love and accept us.

The statistics of the church

Let's pause, take a deep breath, and cover a few needed items before we move on. I want to be careful in my depiction of the church. After all, if the church is not different from the world, the reason for its existence becomes obsolete. Every church should champion strong marriages. Strong families are the cornerstone of any successful society. As the family unit erodes, so does the strength of a society. Is it any wonder then that Satan exerts such great effort toward the tearing apart of our marriages and our families?

Marriage has been ordained by God; He wants to see marriages succeed and the family unit strengthened. After all, God is the one that designed this whole concept of a husband and wife coming together as one, having children, and becoming a family.[25] Therefore, the church should do all they can to strengthen and build up this family unit ordained and blessed by God. Statistics show that the church is making a difference in this area. In his book, *Christian Are Hate-Filled Hypocrites…and Other Lies You've Been Told*, Bradley R. E. Wright found that 60 percent of those who identified as Christians but rarely attended church were divorced. However, of those Christians who attended church regularly, only 38 percent were divorced.[26] This tells us that regular church attendance leads to stronger and more successful marriages. Therefore, the church is making a difference.

While 38 percent is much less than 60 percent, we still see that almost four in every ten people within the church are divorced. In this area, the mission field has been brought to the front door of the church. The question must be asked, "What is the church doing to minister to this 38 percent of members within its own body?"

Over the next several pages, you will notice a shift taking place in this book. The previous eight chapters have been written directly to the person who is currently walking through the difficult valley of

---

[25] Matthew 19:4–6
[26] Bradley R. E. Wright, *Christians Are Hate-Filled Hypocrites…and Other Lies You've Been Told*, (Minneapolis, MN: Bethany House, 2010), p. 133.

divorce. While there is great understanding to be gained by others who are simply reading about this valley, those *experiencing* it were the target audience. This section of the book, "The Church," is not written to the separated or divorced individual. Again, there is great understanding, comfort, and help that can be found for them within these chapters, but this section is written directly to "the church." If we, the church, are going to minister effectively to the nearly 40 percent of members that frequent our services, we must first be able to see them as Christ sees them and our hearts must hurt for them. The mission field is at your front door. Are you willing to open your door and minister to them?

CHAPTER 10

How Will the Church View Me?

As people who love Him, I feel like we tend to let religion and laws rule over relationships and loving people where they are.

—Alissa

The church was a rock to me at the time.

—Mark

God blesses those who mourn, for they will be comforted.

—*Matthew 5:4 NLT*

Mark's story

Mark loved music. So much so that Mark played in the worship band at church. When any kind of guitar is placed into Mark's hands, something magical begins to happen. Despite being involved in music ministry, Mark knew his marriage was on the rocks. He wanted to save his marriage, but over time, it became obvious that the marriage was going to end.

As his marriage fell apart behind closed doors, it was only a matter of time before it became very public. It was during this period that the music minister and the associate pastor came to Mark, knowing his situation, and told him that they felt he should take a step back from his ministry position. Even though it was a difficult decision, Mark understood and agreed.

Don's story

Don had a similar story. His separation happened quickly. It even blindsided him. "I worried about what my place would be in ministry." Don said, "Would I be accepted or not?" Don was co-pastoring at the time. Now he found himself in a leadership position facing a very public challenge. What should he do? "As soon as I found out that she was divorcing me, I immediately resigned from the church. That was a difficult call to make," Don recalled.

Susan's story

Susan was not in a position in the church where she was "up front." However, her ex-husband had been. Now Susan found herself dreading the first time she went back to church. As the worship time began, Susan, standing near the back, found herself crying while she tried to sing. It was at that time that the "sound guy left his post," came down to Susan, hugged her, and told her he loved her. Then he made his way back to the sound booth. That one small act of kindness brought about a peace in Susan's heart. In her mind, she thought, *It's going to be okay.*

Alissa's story

Alissa went through a process that many of us can relate to. "I felt like they felt badly toward me. I began to project what I was feeling according to how they were viewing me, which was probably not right… I felt judged. I was writing their viewpoint, and I would say, nine times out of ten, it was never even the case. But that's the devil. It's a tool he uses, especially when he uses a failure in our lives. I felt like a failure. I felt like it was my fault. I felt like I didn't make it work, even though I know for a fact that there was not one more thing I could have done." The day had come when God had given Alissa peace. "But then," Alissa said, "I stole my own peace by trying to write what everybody else's opinions of me were because I was divorced." What was Alissa's response to this internal turmoil? She began to pull away from church. "I wouldn't commit to going to church. I would go very sparsely," she said. "I still was deeply having a relationship with Jesus…but I needed to be away from the prying eyes. That's how I felt. It didn't mean it was reality, but it was definitely how I felt."

My story

I remember coming home to the church that I had grown up in. Fortunately, due to COVID-19, our services were drive-in services. I would ride to church with my parents and then sit quietly in the back seat, hoping not to attract any attention. I was surrounded by some of the best people on the planet, but I did not know if they knew. If they did know, I wondered what they were thinking about me. That back seat also offered some anonymity as a song or spoken word would often cause tears to begin forming in my eyes. My heart hurt so badly, but I was afraid to let others know.

Tami's story

For Tami, her experience was a little different. She was now on her second marriage and desperately wanted to make it work. "I just didn't want to have a second failed marriage," she recalled. Even though she was in an abusive relationship, she didn't want her marriage to fall apart. One Sunday morning, on her way out of church, Tami asked the pastor to pray for her husband. Her pastor responded, "What I am praying for is for you to let go gracefully." This shocked Tami. How could a pastor be praying for her to have peace in leaving a relationship?

To the church

Today, divorce has become a harsh reality of our society. Books could be, and have been, written about why this is the case. Countless books have been written about how to save your marriage. Scores of books have been written about when it is right, if ever, to divorce and remarry. However, the fact still remains that divorce happens. It has happened to people you know, to close friends, and probably even to loved ones within your own family. If your church can say that there is no one who has been divorced within your congregation, I would have to respond that your church is failing to reach your community.

We have seen a shift, especially within the more conservative church world, over the last twenty-five years. There was a time that a divorced person was ostracized within the church. Beth recalls such a time in her own life. At the time of Beth's separation from her husband, they had pretty much stopped going to church. After the divorce, Beth began making an effort to get back to church. She began attending services at her former house of worship. The church was in the middle of a search for a new pastor. Beth recalls the day when one potential pastor tried out for the new position. Afterward, during a question-and-answer time, someone asked him, "What place would anyone who has been divorced have in your church?" The potential pastor responded, "They would not have a place. They can't do anything [referring to ministry roles]." This one statement almost caused Beth to, once again, leave the church. Fortunately, the pastor was not hired at her church.

Today, the church as a whole, possibly out of necessity, has become more accepting of divorced people within their congregation and often within their leadership. Some of you will agree with these changes, and others will not. However, I simply say this to point out that the church world seems to be at a point where they are generally accepting of the divorced person, but they seem to be lost in knowing how to minister to this demographic.

Every story above has a common thread. Each of us came into a familiar church setting. We knew many of the people around us. We were very well acquainted with the beliefs, customs, and teachings of that particular church. In the past, it had been a place of comfort for us. When we were there, we were in our "comfort zone." Now, something major had changed in our lives. The place that used to make us feel good and comfortable now brought feelings of doubt, fear, and stress into our hearts.

"There was such a deep fear of being divorced," Alissa recalled. "It was probably my biggest obstacle. It was the fact that I would have 'divorce' associated with myself and that I had failed. I felt like I failed my husband, I failed God, and I failed myself by being divorced." Beth expressed a similar feeling. "I think most of the rejection that I felt was more inside. I don't think anybody rejected me per se. I felt ashamed and so there were certain people that I just pulled away from."

Divorce differs from every other "failure" in this way. Every other public failure in our lives is generally easily defined. Someone commits adultery; therefore, they are an adulterer. Someone has committed murder; therefore, they are a murderer. Someone has robbed their neighbor; therefore, they are a thief. Someone sets fire to another's house or property; therefore, they are an arsonist.

Sunday morning comes, and through the doors of your church walks someone who has recently been separated from their spouse. What label are you going to attach to that person? Maybe they committed adultery, or maybe their spouse was unfaithful to them. Maybe they have been physically or verbally abused in private for years, and you never knew anything was happening. Maybe their spouse simply chose to leave them, and now they find themselves in a position they never dreamed they would be in. You may know bits and pieces of their story, but you do not know all of it.

There is one thing you can know. That person that just walked into your sanctuary is hurting tremendously. They are filled with fear of what you or someone else might say to them. Underneath that thin veil of a smile that covers their face is a dam holding back the floodgate of tears about to burst in response to one unkind word or condescending look. That person may look the same on the outside as they did last week or last month, but their insides are churning with a mixture of fears, hurts, and emotions that are raw and real. Their world has been destroyed, and their future looks unspeakably uncertain.

You probably crawled out of bed this morning and came to church simply out of habit. For the separated spouse that now scans the room for a friendly face, standing in the doorway of that sanctuary is an act of courage that would rival a brave firefighter rushing into a burning building seeking to save a life. *What happens in the next ninety minutes could well determine whether that person will ever darken the doorway of your church again.* Then it happens. Their searching eyes see you looking at them. The mission field is looking right at you; what are you going to do about it?

The dilemma

Mark stepped back from his leadership position in the band at church until he could get his life back on track. Even though the assistant pastor and music minister had asked Mark to do this, they also made sure he understood that they were not rejecting him. "I don't think that a week went by that I didn't have pretty much every member of the band, the associate pastor, and my music minister contacting me and asking if I needed anything," Mark recalled. "There were several times they would say, 'Hey, let's just go get something to drink. Let's go get some ice cream.' They all came alongside me." Even though leadership felt like Mark needed some time away, they went out of their way to make sure he knew that they cared, and they walked beside Mark during the most difficult time in his life.

As you look at that hurting person that is looking back at you, Satan begins to hurl a thousand thoughts in your direction. *Just look away and walk away*, you think. *After all, I don't know that person all that well. They probably aren't even thinking about it. I don't want to bring it back to their minds.* All these thoughts have a common theme: avoidance. Rather than going to the one who hurts, we fear saying the wrong thing or bringing up an unwanted topic, so we simply stay away. Don remembers, "Some people, I think, may have known about it and didn't want to go there, so they stayed away from me or didn't bring it up."

"The mentality within the church is that we don't talk about it," stated Alissa. "It happened. You grieve it privately, and you go on with life. I felt like, as the church, we are failing our people. We are failing humanity by covering up and not being open." But what happens if you go and talk to that person and they aren't thinking about it? you ask. "You're *always* thinking about it," Susan recalls, "and sometimes people need to talk about it."

Inside the mind of every recently separated or divorced person that enters through the doors of your church are two questions: (1) Do they know about my current situation? and (2) What are they thinking about me? There is a great amount of fear wrapped up in those two questions. You can greatly reduce that fear by a smile, a kind word, and a simple sentence like "I know what you are going through, and I believe in you." During a normal time in life, those words may seem simple, but to a person walking through the valley of divorce, you have just given them the hope and confidence to make it through another day. Don't walk away; a simple word can make a tremendous impact.

CHAPTER 11

Help or Hinder?

The devil knows the Bible better than you
do. He uses the Bible. He uses God to
hurt God's people all the time by giving
you wrong stigmas and wrong ideas.

—Alissa

I wished that people realized how hard it
was to be alone and not let you be alone.

—Tami

*So encourage each other and build each
other up, just as you are already doing.*

—*1 Thessalonians 5:11 NLT*

Mark's story continues

The day came when Mark's associate pastor asked him if he wanted to say anything to the congregation. It was about to become very clear to the church body that something had happened. Mark availed himself of the opportunity. "I didn't go into any detail," Mark recalled. "I just said there are things happening in my life, and I just need your prayer, your understanding, and your support." After Mark finished speaking, he was amazed by the number of people who came forward and "enveloped" him. The church became "a rock" to Mark. "Almost all were very supportive," Mark remembers. "They didn't even want to know details. They didn't want to know how or why. They just wanted me to know that I was loved."

Can you imagine the fears in Mark's mind that began to dissolve as people came forward and encircled him? Can you feel the hurts that began to heal during this time? The corporate support that Mark received from his church must be similar to what Paul was advocating for in Galatians 6:2 when he wrote, "Bear ye one another's burdens, and so fulfill the law of Christ."

"I no longer felt all alone," Mark stated. "I'm still in church today because my church family reflected Jesus to me in a very real way."

Individual hindrances

It would be great if everyone's story was like Mark's. In a perfect church world, filled with perfect Christians, everyone would say the right words and do the right things, and the church would be known worldwide as a hospital for the hurting. However, all too often, individuals within the church take a different approach.

Tami recalls a friend at church telling her, "You know, you can never remarry."

"It was hurtful," Tami said. "To even be at church was a struggle. I had to get two kids ready. I didn't want to be there. I just wanted to sit at home." In the midst of her struggle for survival, someone felt it necessary to make sure Tami knew that this loneliness and pain she was feeling would be permanent because her fate had been sealed.

Less than a year after Tami's divorce, she was driving home from church. All of a sudden, she felt what she describes as a "shift" happening within her. Tami immediately felt a peace inside. She thought, *I'm okay. Thank you, Jesus. I'm okay.* "I feel like God came and gave me a touch—a healing," she recalled. The very next Sunday, a well-meaning lady came up to Tami and gave her a stack of cards with scripture verses written on them.

"You need to pray these over [your ex-husband]," the lady told Tami.

"Well, I think God is helping me to let go," Tami responded.

"No, you can't do that," retorted the lady, "you need to pray these over him and get your marriage back."

The marriage had been an abusive one from which Tami had now found freedom. However, Tami reluctantly took the cards and began reading them and praying. "I just ended up right back where I was," Tami remembers. The peace that Tami had felt had now vanished. "I, to this day, feel that she yanked me back from a gift of God," stated Tami.

Less than a year after Alissa's divorce, her ex-husband began trying to work his way back into her life. One day, Alissa was sitting in church listening to the sermon. "An audible voice said to me," Alissa recalled, "and said, 'If you pick up what I freed you from, I won't free you again.' It shook me. It scared me." A few days later, her ex-husband came into her work and again insisted they get back together. "I gave my heart back to God," Alissa told him. "To get to me, you have to talk to Him." Within a week, it was clear that Alissa had made the correct decision.

For some, the thought of God "freeing" someone from their ex-spouse or the Holy Spirit telling someone to not go back doesn't fit into your theology. That's fine. How God chooses to work and deal with a person struggling through a separation and divorce is not dependent upon your theology. Today, in the church world, we all too often find Christians who are more interested in trying to do the convicting work of the Holy Spirit than they are with being the hands and feet of Jesus.

Someone going through a divorce does not need your shame cast upon them. They are already experiencing shame. They are already aware of how they look to the church world. They know what they did or didn't do wrong. A person going through a divorce is in need of a church of believers who will circle around them, support them, and, like the Holy Spirit, walk beside them during quite possibly the deepest valley they will ever experience.

Individual help

As in the story of Mark's church, it is not very hard to go forward with several other people and show support for a struggling individual. Is that enough though? When that individual goes home, who will support them there? Again, we come back to this battle of wanting to do the right thing but not knowing what to do. "I think people just don't know what to say. I don't think they know what to do," stated Alissa. "They will say, 'I'm praying for you and I love you,' but there aren't people coming and getting into the trenches with you and saying, 'Hey, I'm going to bring supper,' or 'I'm going to take you out, do you want to go?' 'I'm just going to listen to you talk,' that's what I feel like the body should do. The body didn't do that for me." Alissa then pondered, "People did care, they did reach out." However, she continued, "I feel like, as the body of Christ, we failed people."

Tami remembers a similar experience. "I don't remember being invited to anyone's house for a meal. I don't remember anyone in my church calling and saying, 'Do you have plans?'"

Sometimes, a small act of kindness can mean so much. Susan recalls a time, shortly into her separation, when such an act had a great impact. Susan hadn't been sleeping well as she struggled with the fear of an empty house. One of the older ladies in the church knew that Susan was struggling to find rest. One day, this lady called Susan and said, "Tonight you are going to sleep because I am going to spend the night praying for you." Susan continued, "That night, I slept better than I ever had." This one act of kindness and sacrifice meant the world to Susan.

For Tami, that act of kindness was displayed in an act of confidence. After Tami's divorce, the pastoral intern came to her and said, "Tami, I want you to start a ministry with the college kids. I want you to have them over to your house and give them a snack, play games, and fellowship." Initially, Tami turned the intern down. *I don't have energy for that*, Tami thought. After all, she spent a lot of time at home crying. How was she going to handle a dozen college kids in her house when she could hardly manage to care for her two small children?

The intern persisted because he saw she was sinking and needed purpose. Tami reluctantly agreed. Looking back on that interaction, Tami now says, "It saved me." There were two things this did for her. First, it forced her to clean her house weekly. This hadn't been the case previously as Tami suffered from emotional exhaustion. Secondly, for a few hours every Sunday night, her house was filled with noise, food, fun, and laughter.

One Sunday morning, Tami simply didn't show up for church. Two of those college kids came to her house and began banging on her door. They knew Tami was home and kept knocking until she finally came and answered the door. "I insisted I was fine," Tami said. "Well, I don't know what is going on," one of them responded, "but if you are not at church tonight, we will be back." This act of confidence that the intern showed in Tami and her reluctant willingness to accept his request built bonds between her and some college kids that still remain, even to this day.

One day, Alissa was grappling with the idea of getting divorced. Her marriage was abusive, and others were telling Alissa to get out; but she continued to carry on in the marriage, waiting on God to free her from the marriage. One day, while Alissa was struggling with this decision, one of the ladies from her church came into Alissa's office at work. Even though they did not know each other well, Alissa began to tell this lady about this journey she had been on. The lady told her, "I'm going to pray for you every day." This lady began to lift Alissa up in intercessory prayer on a daily basis.

She also began to send Alissa postcards in the mail. Each postcard is a solid color on the front. On the back, the lady simply writes a scripture verse that God had given her to share with Alissa. "It is amazing," Alissa recalls, "that when I am at my lowest times, I will often go to the mailbox and will find a postcard from this lady with the scripture verse that I need to hear." Some weeks, Alissa will receive one postcard in the mail; other weeks, it may be two or more. It has been four years since that conversation at work, and the lady continues to pray daily for Alissa and send her postcards with handwritten scripture verses on them.

What can I do?

The stories above are just a few examples of what to do to show a person going through a divorce that you care. For many, the lack of reaching out is not due to a lack of love but rather a lack of knowledge. So what should you do?

"People didn't know what to say. They didn't know what to do," recalled Alissa. "It wasn't a matter of not being there for me. It was a matter of not knowing *how* to be there. Sometimes it is just a matter of being there for people. You don't have to know all the answers."

Susan advises, "Just be with them. You don't necessarily have to say anything. Bring them food. Send a card. A call means so much. Just don't ignore them."

"I know what I wished," Tami recalls. "I wished that people wouldn't let me be alone. Don't let people be alone. Don't let them be alone. It's a burden, I guess, but just reach out and make sure people are not alone."

Don's advice to Christians: "Recognize the pain. Recognize the loneliness." Let them know. "I know your heart hurts. I want you to know that it's going to get better. You are going to heal, and there is going to come a day when you don't feel that pain anymore."

Don't forget the children

For a brief moment you look away, then after a few seconds, you look up and see that hurting person making their way to your pew. For the first time, you notice a little one grasping the hand of that mother or father. In an instant, you come to the realization that this separation is affecting many more people than just the two going through it. There are children involved.

For some reason, our society, the church included, rarely comes to the aid of the children when the parents are going through a separation and divorce. We don't see the intense pain and loss of identity that these children are facing. Please note, this child may be two years old or forty-two years old, but the hurt is still real. In the next section of the book, "The Children of Divorce," you will meet many children of divorce, including Sheena. She was a senior in high school when her parents separated and her father moved out. "I wish someone from the church would have stepped in and taken on the role of a father in my life," Sheena lamented. "I wish a lady in the church would have stepped up as a mother and showed me how to mature into a godly woman."

The role of the church is not just to help the hurting parent but also to rally around the child. In James 1:27, we read about the most genuine display of religion. It reads, "Pure religion and undefiled before God and the Father is this, to visit the fatherless and widows in their affliction, and to keep himself unspotted from the world" (KJV). Is "the fatherless" simply talking about a child whose father has died, or could it be speaking of children whose father is no longer in their lives? Is a widow only someone who has lost her husband to death, or could a widow be someone who has lost her husband to an affair or to drugs or alcohol?

The church has a great responsibility to come alongside that hurting man or woman who has lost their spouse to anything, not just death. The church also must begin to realize the pain caused to the children of divorce and become a father and mother to the "fatherless" of any aged children that darken our church doors.

Conclusion

Dear church, please listen. Your mission field has moved into your pew. You may not know their story, but you are aware of their situation. Beside you is someone who is silently crying out for a friend, a listening ear, a kind word, and someone willing to come alongside them. Maybe you didn't know what to do before, but now you do. Reach out! Say a kind word! Do a kind deed! Be that listening ear! Become that father or mother figure that they so desperately need. It may not cost you a dime, but your genuine act could be worth millions to that hurting heart at arm's reach. It's time for the church to become like Jesus and walk beside those who are deeply hurting.

SECTION 4

The Children of Divorce

> Your whole identity is built around your parents when you are young. When all of the sudden that's taken away, what happens now? It swept my foundation away.
>
> —Jon

> *Ye are of God, little children, and have overcome them: because greater is He that is in you, than He that is in the world.*
>
> —*1 John 4:4 KJV*

The children of divorce

As you find yourself lost in thought and overwhelmed with emotion, your world is suddenly jolted back to reality as you hear a faint but familiar voice entering the room. "Mommy," the voice cries softly, "when is Daddy going to come home?" Those simple words take your shattered heart and break it into a thousand more pieces. How can you answer that question? How can you explain to a child that their mom or dad chose to walk away? You can try to explain that it wasn't because of them, but by our very nature, we are programmed to believe that *I* must have done something wrong to cause another person to abandon me.

Maybe your story is a little different. Instead of that little voice in the room, maybe it was a much deeper voice on the phone. "Dad," says your son, "how could you let this happen? Don't you care about us?" The voice is different, but the words have the same piercing effect. God put you in charge of these young lives, and now, without any intent of doing so, your separation has shattered their world. For a parent, few thoughts can bring more pain than the realization that one of your actions brought hurt to your child.

What will you do in the weeks and months to come to help that child heal? What can you do? What should you do? What shouldn't you do? The realization of this new reality floods over you like a river overflowing its banks. This divorce will not only leave lifelong hurts, memories, and scars on you, but it will have the same effects on your children as well. Whether they are three or thirty-three, their world has just been rocked, and they are totally helpless to do anything to fix it.

As reality sets in, so does the overwhelming desire to take this hurt away from your children, but how? When you find yourself in the depths of a deep valley, how can you find the strength to reach down and pull someone up when you hardly have the strength to carry yourself? Possibly more than ever before, your children are looking to you for comfort, wisdom, strength, and stability. How are you going to respond?

Chapter 12

The Children of Divorce

> I don't believe we think, sometimes, when
> we are going through a divorce about
> how much it affects those we love.
>
> —Alissa

> I compared myself to other kids at
> school. I knew I was different.
>
> —Derek

A father to the fatherless, a defender of widows,
is God in His holy dwelling.

—Psalm 68:5 NIV

Shelby's story

It was a warm Friday in early June. I was a youth pastor at the time, and we were in the midst of Vacation Bible School. That afternoon, I received a text from Shelby. "I need to talk to you, it's urgent," she texted. I arranged to meet Shelby at the church a little before the time VBS was to begin. Shelby had been in my youth group and, having just graduated from high school, was preparing to head off for college. She was always happy and bubbly.

I arrived at the church and met Shelby. As she started to talk, she burst into tears. "My dad cheated on my mom, and mom says she's done. My parents are going to get a divorce." The words hit me like a load of bricks. I knew her parents well. How could this be happening? As Shelby cried, she continued to give me more details about the situation. In one day, her world had been shattered.

Kids and divorce

Shelby's story is one that millions of kids could tell. Oh sure, this detail or that detail would be different, but the end result is the same. A child's world has come crashing down because their parents decided to separate. The age of the child really doesn't matter; the effects are still similar. While the parents fight a battle between each other, the child is forced, through no fault of their own, to fight their own battle brought on by the decisions of their parents.

Jon remembers this battle well. He was a preteen when his parents separated. "Your whole identity is built around your parents when you are young," Jon recalls. "When all of the sudden that's taken away, what happens now? It swept my foundation away." Young Jon now lived with his mother and younger siblings. "I was at the age when I needed my dad the most," said Jon. "Dad was the hero, and now he is gone."

For Derek, he was too young to remember his parents getting divorced. The day came, however, when Derek grew older and became aware that his family was not the same as his classmates' families. "I compared myself to other kids at school," Derek said. "I knew I was different." As Derek grew older, he still felt the difference and the distance. "Neither of my parents were the person to go to because they didn't open up to me."

Rachel, while still relatively young, was in the first year of her own marriage when she heard of her parents' impending divorce. "The news came like a huge slap in the face and thereby caused a huge thundercloud over my life. It changed me, my future, and, inevitably, my family's future," Rachel recalls. Rachel knew her parents' marriage was far from perfect but was hopeful that everything would stay as it was, and their little family unit would go on.

Sheena was about to finish her senior year of high school when her mom separated from her dad. "I remember graduation," Sheena recalled, "it was hard. Everyone was tense. I tried talking to my dad, but it wasn't the same." Sheena's mother had led her to believe many bad things about her father. It would be years later before Sheena would discover the truth.

While each of these "children of divorce" vary in age, from a toddler to early twenties, they all experienced similar battles and struggles. Their stories are not unique. Focus on the Family published a study on this subject that revealed some 90 percent of children from divorced homes suffered from an acute sense of shock when the separation occurred, including profound grieving and irrational fears. Fifty percent reported feeling rejected and abandoned. One-third of these children feared abandonment by the remaining parent while almost two-thirds experienced yearning for the absent parent with an intensity that researchers described as overwhelming. In summary, Dr. Nicholi said, "Divorce brings such intense loneliness to children that its pain is difficult to describe or even to contemplate."[27]

The struggle

For a child of divorce, the emotions continue even after the initial shock subsides. "I remember being so sad, thinking that my life will never be the same again," Shelby recalled. "I remember feeling really alone. I was angry that [my dad] couldn't be content."

Jon faced these same internal struggles. "I feel like I lost my identity," Jon recalls. "It was like something I did. It was a feeling of I'm not good enough. That followed me into my thirties."

Sheena knows these feelings well. "I still struggle with who I am. I try to find my identity in God, but it's not easy. I struggle very much with insecurities, the feeling of being alone and abandoned. I feel like I'm not good enough."

---

[27] https://www.dobsonlibrary.com/resource/article/b244d6a1-361a-414a-a49b-ea6470dfe75e

Rachel had similar struggles, but she chose not to face them alone. "I would become an emotional basket case every time we would go visit family because the memories would flood my mind, and Satan would try to take advantage of the circumstances," Rachel said. "I'm so glad for my husband during my parents' divorce, and even now, he has been my rock and helped me through some of the darkest nights when I would cry myself to sleep. He would point me to Jesus when bitterness tried to take over my heart."

For Amber, who was also in her twenties when her parents divorced, she struggled with a battle of beliefs. Amber had been taught her whole life that "divorce is wrong in any capacity unless you are being physically beaten and your life is at risk." Then the very people who had formulated Amber's beliefs on the subject chose to divorce. "My situation with my parents has been shattering," Amber said. "I feel lost in my beliefs of what divorce is or should be."

Taking sides

So often, whether by malicious intent or simply out of anger or ignorance, children are used as pawns, thus making the struggle even more difficult. Amber recalls, "I've been caught in the middle since day one, and I'm currently in therapy trying to deal with everything. It stinks no matter what the age." Sheena stated, "My mom made us take sides." In Rachel's case, her father never talked with her about the marriage or the divorce. "Since I was only hearing one side, it built a resentment towards my dad that stayed with me until my adult years," Rachel remembers. During the divorce process, Rachel "felt like I was trying to hold it all together for me and everyone else." Shelby had similar feelings. At one point, she lamented to her husband, "I'm so tired of parenting my parents."

Staying away

Many times, the real or perceived pressures or struggles at home make it easy to run or simply stay away. Shelby was fortunate in one sense because she was heading away to college. Even though the college was only a couple of hours away and Shelby could have gone home, she generally chose to simply stay away. "I didn't have anywhere to 'go home' to and land."

Jon tried the same approach. "I was being forced to be the caretaker of my younger siblings, which was a job I didn't want, so I didn't come home." He didn't want to be at home, so he found ways and excuses to stay away. "Being in the house was a reminder of everything." The day came when Jon was taken in for observation to find out why he wasn't coming home. "They should have just asked me," Jon said. However, it was during these important early teen years that Jon started getting into trouble.

Rebellion

"I had grandpas and uncles, but nothing replaces a dad," Jon stated, "I spent a lot of time doing things for my dad's attention. When I was a teenager, I learned really quickly that, when I got in trouble, he would show up." Therefore, that is what Jon did. His teenage years were filled with one incident after another. This aimless searching for love and acceptance led Jon to alcohol and even drugs. He went from one unhealthy failed relationship to the next. Eventually, Jon's decisions landed him in jail.

Shelby also became rebellious during her parents' divorce. "I had a terrible time finding a spot where I felt comfortable," Shelby recalled. The day her parents finalized their divorced, Shelby rebelled by getting her lip pierced. Her parents had always forbidden Shelby to get any piercings or tattoos. Now that she was in college and angry at her parents, this was her opportunity to rebel and spite them for hurting her. She knew she would regret a tattoo, so she got her lip pierced instead. However, her plan backfired as neither parent even acknowledged her new piercing. After about a month, Shelby took the lip piercing out as it had not brought her the anger and attention from her parents that she had hoped.

Lingering effects

In the same way that the effects of your divorce continue to linger within you for years to come, children of divorce also continue to struggle with the aftermath of the divorce. Sometimes, some of those struggles are even more difficult for them. "It's hard to watch. It hurts me more that they're hurting," remarked Don. "I've been able to move on, but they still, to some degree, need or continue to have a relationship with their mother. So they can't really move on." This struggle may be why 37 percent of children of divorce reported being even less happy five years after the divorce then they were eighteen months after.[28]

Conclusion

This chapter may have been hard to read for someone going through a separation or divorce. Its purpose was not to defeat you but rather to bring the truth to light as told by those who have watched their parents' divorce. While there are times when divorce is necessary, there are still crushing effects for all those involved, not just the parents. Knowing some of the thoughts and feelings of those "children" who have experienced a divorce, we must now explore the obvious question at hand: how can I help my children through this journey and make it easier for them? Make no mistake, they are walking through the valley of divorce too. So often, however, their journey is overlooked by almost everyone as they struggle to navigate the difficult path unintentionally chosen for them by circumstances out of their control. While others pass by, they are left to themselves to suffer in silence.

---

[28] https://www.dobsonlibrary.com/resource/article/b244d6a1-361a-414a-a49b-ea6470dfe75e

Save the Children

I don't want my kids to go through what
I went through. I'll do whatever it takes
to save them that pain. I'm not going to
push it on my kids. It stops with me.

—Jon

Everything I ever learned about parenting
was from my youth group or friends.
That's not what is supposed to happen.

—Derek

But you, God, see the trouble of the afflicted;
You consider their grief and take it in hand.
The victims commit themselves to You;
You are the helper of the fatherless.

—*Psalm 10:14 NIV*

Mark's story

Mark remembers the night when word of his marital unfaithfulness reached his children. "They were all mad and were all yelling at me. There were a lot of tears and a lot of anger," Mark recalled. As this was transpiring, Mark's teenaged son and youngest child sat quietly through it all. Toward the end of the family confrontation, Mark's son stood up and said, "I'm so mad at you. I would like to punch you in the face. But you are my dad and I love you, and nothing will ever change that." Mark says, "I will never forget that as long as I live."

Even though Mark hoped to save his marriage, it did eventually end in divorce. For Mark's other children, it took time for the hurt and anger to subside before they were willing to begin rebuilding their relationship with their dad. His youngest daughter was the last to come around. The day finally came when his youngest daughter called and began to talk. While she cried, she expressed that the thing that hurt her the most was to realize that her "dad actually was human." She had held him on a high pedestal.

Clearing up confusion

Children, regardless of age, feel many of the same emotions in a divorce as their parents do. They feel the rejection, the hurt, the anger, the loneliness, and so many other emotions. They are hurting, and for many children, their parents are the people they have turned to in the past whenever they are hurt, angry, rejected, or lonely. Now, their world has been turned upside down, and they don't know where to turn.

In addition, many of them feel like Amber when she expressed, "I always felt like I had to choose sides." This insecure feeling can be remedied quickly by mature parents. "There was confusion on the part of my kids," stated Mark. "All four have expressed the idea that they weren't sure how to act because they felt like if they were doing things with their mother, they were betraying me. Likewise, if they were doing something with me, they were betraying their mother." To their credit, both Mark and their mother told the kids, "Do what you want to do with your dad/mom. You are not hurting me. We are just happy that you still care about both of us." This brought great comfort to the kids and relieved some of their fears.

Shelby felt that same comfort as well. "My parents got along from the get-go. Anytime we had a baby shower or a birthday or anything of that nature, they were cordial. They always got along. Mom was always invited to Dad's house. Dad was always invited whenever we would go and do anything. It was really a blessing for us. It took a ton of stress off of us. I don't think they ever stopped thinking of one another as family."

Back in chapter 1, we talked about the hurt that comes when you are rejected by someone in your family. That hurt is multiplied proportionally depending on the depth of love for that person. As the old saying goes, "There is a fine line between love and hate." The hurt felt by a child of divorce causes very strong feelings because of the depth of their love for their parents. Therefore, your child might express strong feelings of anger, bitterness, and hurt toward you during this time. How you handle the process will go a long way in building or destroying your future relationship with your child.

Advice for parents

As a parent, you have a big task as you try to help your child navigate this difficult path. "The parents are key to healing their children during the process," says Alissa. "You have to be honest and open, and you have to point them up [to Jesus]." So how can you help your child heal? Here are some suggestions from those who have gone through it.

"Really open lines of communication are key between the child and the parent," stated Shelby. Rachel felt the same way. "I would appreciate or would have appreciated talking about it more." Rachel continued, "The parent should ask their child if they have questions, what they're going through, and how they can help them instead of avoiding the situation or pretending like everything is okay. They still have to be the parent and the mature one in the situation."

This communication needs to be positive as well. "Do not talk badly about the other parent to your child," advised Rachel. Shelby went a step further. "Don't talk badly about the other parent to the child or within earshot of the child, like on the phone to a friend. It certainly helps to be civil towards the other parent in front of the child as well," stated Rachel. "If the child asks questions," noted

Sheena, "answer their questions but in a loving way. Don't talk badly about the other parent."

So often, an adult child will become almost like a peer to a parent. Sometimes, this relationship will cause the parent to go to their child for advice and support. "Do not lean on your child as your emotional support," advised Rachel. "The children, even if they're adults, are still the children in this situation and should not be expected to 'parent' their parents." Instead, Rachel suggested, "The parent should find a trustworthy, godly person of the same gender for advice and support during that time."

Lastly, find a parenting plan that works. Shelby suggested, "Be very 'cut-and-dry' on when the kids will be with the other parent, especially on holidays. It was hard for me to try and figure out who to be with on holidays." Shelby continued, "Be flexible with the parenting plan. If the kid wants to go to a birthday party…let them."

Conclusion

Every child of divorce I interviewed spoke in one way or another about the selfishness of divorce. Children are taught at a young age to share, get along, be kind, and love others. They then see one or both of their parents doing what they taught them not to do. When you are going through this process, put great value in your relationship with your child and in their relationship with the other parent. Each unkind word you say to your child about their mother or father chisels one more piece away from their foundation at a time when they need it the most. Remember, they are children, regardless of their age. Do your best to love and support them during this difficult time. The day will come when your maturity during your divorce will bring about great rewards in your relationship with your children and in their own growth and healing.

Chapter 14

Redemption

> What has happened in your past
> doesn't have to be your future.
>
> —Shelby

> It was in coming to Christ that I realized I
> did not need others' acceptance. Christ is
> my identity that I lost when I was a kid.
>
> —Jon

> *But in my distress, I cried out to the L*ORD*;*
> *yes, I prayed to my God for help.*
> *He heard me from His sanctuary;*
> *my cry to Him reached His ears.*
>
> —*Psalm 18:6 NLT*

Eleese's story

Eleese was one year old when Alissa made the difficult decision to separate from Eleese's dad. At the time, Eleese was too young to understand, but after a couple of years, she began to realize that she did not have a dad like the other kids. Eleese also knew that her father was African American. She began to feel that void in her life and made it her little mission to find her father. Wherever she went, if she saw a

Man of Color, she would walk up to him and ask, "Are you my dad?" This led to many embarrassing situations for her mother, Alissa.

When Eleese would ask about her daddy, Alissa would respond by saying something like, "Your daddy loves you." One day, Alissa's counselor told Alissa to stop saying that. "You are telling her that her daddy loves her, but yet he chose a different life and chose to walk away. You are teaching her that that is love." Alissa realized the harm in teaching that. Instead Alissa started telling her young daughter, "I know you want a dad, but Jesus is your heavenly Father, and He will hold you until God sees fit to give you the earthly father that He will give you." Eleese was content with this answer.

Strengthened marriages

Although there are many negative effects of divorce on children, there may be one that is a positive. While it is a small sample size, those I interviewed generally responded that their parents' divorce made them more determined to have a better marriage. "I feel like I am more cautious of everything," responded Shelby. "Marriage is really fragile and you have to protect it. If you are not careful, there are outside sources that are constantly trying to break it down, and you have to guard it. I want to be stronger and not give in to those outside sources."

Rachel remarked, "My parents' divorce has made me more intentional in my own marriage. I will never put my children through what my parents put me through." Amber feels the same way. "Honestly," she says, "my parents' divorce makes me fight harder for mine." Even though Derek isn't married yet, he feels this same determination. "I would love to know that I would be together with my spouse forever, till we die," he said.

The main negative mentioned dealt with trust. Shelby remarked, "If my husband were to ever do something to break my trust, I think I would really, really struggle." Jon spoke of a difficulty to trust as well. "My trust was broken," Jon said. "When your trust is broken, it is very hard to replace that." Marriage, maybe more so than any relationship, is founded on trust. When a child has watched that trust broken in their parents, they feel the effects of that, and it is only natural to believe that they would worry about this in their own marriage.

Shelby's story continues

After several years apart, Shelby's dad began emailing and pursuing Shelby's mom. Shelby describes her mother as "a very forgiving person." For Shelby, these new developments brought about a sense of hope that it would make her life easier but hesitant in a sense that it would totally break her heart if it happened again. Most of all, she feared how it would affect her children if Grandma and Grandpa "were together and then not together again."

"Long story short," Shelby said, "I feel like our lives just meshed together." Her parents had been cordial and had always gotten along, even after the divorce, so the road back together was a short one. Shelby's parents began "dating" again and were soon reunited in marriage. "The feeling of togetherness whenever they got back together was apparent to all of us," Shelby recalled. "Everyone felt complete. That's how it's supposed to be. It was really good."

Only about 10 to 15 percent of divorced couples eventually get back together.[29] However, when it does happen, the effects on the children can be quite positive. When Shelby was asked, "What has it meant to have your parents come back together and your family reunited?" She, with a content smile on her face, responded, "I wish everyone could have it. Complete: that's the only way I can describe it. I definitely feel that God had a hand in it."

Advice for children

Having experienced her parents' divorce, Shelby offers advice to other children of divorce. "You will get through this," she says. "Time does heal a lot of things. Most of all, your parents' divorce doesn't have to be your story. You write your own story. What has happened in the past doesn't have to be your future."

---

[29] https://www.jonnyklaw.com/blog/2020/february

Jon wants other children of divorce to know that "you are somebody. It's not your fault." Sheena agrees and adds, "Don't blame yourself. Be yourself. You don't have to hide. Find someone you can trust to talk to. Don't hold it in." Most of all, Sheena exhorts, "Hold on to God. He will never forsake you."

Your heavenly Father

The Bible often speaks of Jesus as our "heavenly Father." For someone like myself that grew up with a godly earthly father, grasping the concept of a caring heavenly Father is not difficult. For a child who has never known their father or has not known the love of their earthly father, this concept becomes much more difficult to grasp. For years, Jon struggled to find acceptance from his earthly father. Even into his marriage, Jon was still looking for acceptance and was struggling with his identity. That all changed the day Jon truly accepted Christ not only as his Father but also his Savior. "It was in coming to Christ that I realized I did not need others' acceptance," Jon recalled. "Christ is my identity that I lost when I was a kid."

Sheena has experienced similar feelings. "When my parents were going through their separation and ultimately divorced, I started putting up walls to protect myself. It was a wall to protect my heart," Sheena recalls. These walls continue to plague her today, even in other relationships. "I struggle fully trusting God and other people because of my lack of trust in my parents. I have a relationship with God but struggle to go deeper into that relationship because of those walls."

Putting up walls to protect yourself from the pain, hurt, and rejection of a toxic relationship is sometimes necessary. After all, Proverbs 4:23 (NLT) does say, "Guard your heart above all else for it determines the course of your life." What happens, though, when that erected wall, due to the broken trust of a parent, hinders our relationship with God? Trust is easily broken but often very difficult to restore. In order to experience true and total healing, one must experience firsthand a relationship with Christ as their heavenly Father.

Maybe the answer is found a couple verses later in Proverbs 4:25–26 (NLT). Here we read, "Look straight ahead, and fix your eyes on what lies before you. Mark out a straight path for your feet; stay on the safe path." The pain of hurt and rejection causes us to fix our eyes in the past. We often obsess about the difficult journey we have traveled, rather than fixing our eyes on what lies ahead.

That path ahead may look difficult, but Proverbs 3:5–6 (NLT) gives us the keys and the answers we seek. "Trust in the Lord with all your heart; do not depend on your own understanding. Seek His will in all you do, and He will show you which path to take." You may not understand why your parents' divorce happened. However, you can rest assured that God knows, and He sees and cares about you. You may struggle to trust others, but the Bible instructs us to trust in the Lord with *all* your heart. Why? Because God has promised "I will never fail you. I will never abandon you."[30] When you seek His will in all you do, "He will show you which path to take." The path behind you may be filled with scars, but the path before you can be a new and bright beginning. Guard your heart against evil and against those who would seek to hurt you; but trust God with it, and He will lead you in a new direction.

Eleese's story continues

After Alissa began pointing her daughter to Jesus as her heavenly Father, Eleese began to grasp the concept and would often repeat, "God is my heavenly daddy." Her mother responds, "Yes, He is." When Eleese was four years old, she again said to her mother, "God is my heavenly daddy?" Alissa responded, "Yes, He is." This time, however, Eleese asked, "Can I go sit on His lap? I just want to hug Him."

"It wrecked me as a mom," Alissa said with tears streaming down her face, "that she does not have a father to climb up on his lap and to love her and to take her on dates and to show her how a man is to love a woman and be a father and a husband."

---

[30] Hebrews 13:5 (NLT)

One day, Alissa was driving home from work weeping as she pondered how her daughter would not have a father like she had. At that moment, she felt God say to her, "Alissa, that was your story. It's not Eleese's story. I have a different journey for her. Her frame is built for something different than yours." Alissa remembers the peace she felt as God said, "I'm going to heal her, and I am going to make sure I fill those voids in her life, and that they are used for what I have planned for her and for the people she will encounter. Your journey is not your daughter's."

Conclusion

Whatever your past, whatever your story, whatever your journey, you can rest assured that God can use it for good. When our earthly parents fail us, God steps up even more to fill that void. Rachel recalls, "There was a time when I was so disappointed in both of my earthly parents that I related more as God's child than as my parents'. I suppose maybe we're supposed to feel that way. He is the perfect parent. He will never disappoint. His grace and peace are what saved me through the lowest points of my life, through my parent's divorce."

Whether you are a child of divorce or a divorced parent with children, the answer is the same. Trust God. Crawl up into His lap and let Him wrap His arms around you. No one else will write your story. Your past does not determine your future. Allow God to fill those voids in your life. Find your identity and worth in Him. He will heal your hurts, and He can take your story and turn it into something beautiful. You are no longer identified as a child of divorce. From now on, your identity is found in being a child of God.

SECTION 5

Cultivating Healing

You have to allow God to heal you; and you
have to allow yourself to let that happen.

—Tami

*So be strong and courageous! Do not be afraid
and do not panic before them. For the Lord
your God will personally go ahead of you, He
will neither fail you nor abandon you.*

—*Deuteronomy 31:6 (NLT)*

Cultivating healing

Some time has passed. It may be a month; it may be a year, but you feel something begin to come to life within you. It is that feeling you get when you see the first signs of your garden beginning to sprout. A seed was planted weeks before. You have watered the ground, removed the weeds that try to come up, and made sure to give that seed and dirt plenty of sunlight. One day, you look and see just a touch of green coming up from the ground. It's not like the weeds before it. No, this little leaf is different. For the first time, you see just the smallest proof that your work was not in vain. You know this is not the end but rather the beginning. That little leaf will require more care over the next several weeks, but there is now evidence that it exists.

As you look at that ever-so-tiny plant, your mind begins to wonder: *Why today? Why didn't it sprout yesterday, or why not tomorrow? What makes today so special?* Then you ask the question: *What makes this plant so special?* After some thought, you realize that you are looking at new life, and with that comes hope. It may be small now, but you know, if you cultivate the ground around it and give it the water, sunlight, and nutrition it needs, it will one day become something strong and beautiful.

It is so easy to want to see that seed become a beautiful flower or a delicious watermelon or a strong and glorious tree, but all these things require one difficult ingredient—*time*. Life would be so wonderful if you could put that seed in the soil today and be eating the watermelon or picking the rose tomorrow. However, growth requires time. There is one other thing that growth requires. It must have a starting point.

Are you ready to grow? Then it's time to cultivate the ground and plant the seed.

Chapter 15

Hope

This isn't a mountain to climb. I just
have to get through today.

—Don

When there was no pain, I took joy in other things.

—Susan

*Rejoice in our confident hope. Be patient
in trouble, and keep on praying.*

—*Romans 12:12 NLT*

Don's story

Don's life had been a roller coaster since the day his wife left. Weeks had passed, and Don wanted nothing more than to heal and to move on. He would do good for two or three days and then a memory or a picture or something else would trigger him, and he would have a bad day. "I was in tears constantly. I couldn't sleep, and my heart hurt. I felt like I was trying to make it over this mountain," Don recalled. "I would make it three steps forward and then two steps back. I was beginning to feel despair because I didn't feel like I could get to the top."

One day, Don shared this struggle and these feelings with a friend who had come alongside Don soon after the separation. This friend knew the struggle because he had walked this valley a decade before. "Don, that's not reality," his friend explained. "Your journey is not a climb over a mountain but rather a linear path. Some days you are down. Some days you are up. But the further away you get from the incident, the further apart the down times are, and the shallower the down times become."

"That helped me tremendously," Don said. "Each day that passes I'm getting further away from the point of impact. My low spots will get higher and my high spots will get higher." Armed with this information, Don had a whole new perspective on his healing journey. By simply shifting his focus, Don had been given a powerful gift in healing. He now had *hope*.

Susan's story

Shortly after Susan's husband left, she had dinner with another woman who had walked this same path.

Susan asked her, "How long will it be before I wake up and this is not the first thing I think of and the last thing I think of before I go to bed?"

The woman responded, "It will happen faster than you realize."

A few weeks later, Susan was walking down the hallway where she taught. The sun was shining brightly through the window. "I just remember my heart filled with anticipation for the future," Susan recalled. "I remember feeling happy for the first time." There was nothing overly special about that day, but that was the day that a little green leaf from the seed of hope came up from the soil and sprouted. Susan's healing had begun.

Hindrances to healing

Anyone going through the valley of divorce longs for that healing to take place as quickly as possible. During the darkest days, it is difficult to see a day in the future when one could truly be happy and feel optimism and anticipation for what lies ahead. However, that day will come. How quickly it comes depends largely upon your situation and your willingness to begin that healing process.

It should be pointed out that each person's journey is different. There is no cookie-cutter time line to how long it will take for healing. If you were married for twenty-five years with three kids, logic would tell you that your recovery will take longer than someone married for one year with no children. If due to the children or location you still see your former spouse on a consistent basis, those wounds are going to take longer to heal.

Another factor that can hinder our healing is our desire to hold on to the past. Tami explained this in her life. "I impeded my own healing because I felt like, if I truly loved [my ex-husband] I wouldn't be healed. If I allowed God to heal me, somehow in my mind that meant I didn't really love [my ex-husband]." Today, Tami can see the error in her thinking. "[The hurt and pain] truly can go away," Tami now says, "but you have to allow God to heal you, and you have to allow yourself to be healed."

For years, Beth struggled to heal because she struggled to reconcile what was real in her marriage and what was fake. The day arrived when Beth came to the realization, "Whatever was real in my head is real, and whatever was going on behind my back, that's on him." She continued, "So if I have good memories of certain things that we did, that's real." Coming to terms with this in her mind allowed Beth to stop looking at the past and begin focusing on the future.

The last major obstacle to healing is bitterness. While that other person no longer lives in your home, it is quite easy to give them free rent in your head. This can lead to bitterness and a longing for revenge. The Bible, however, gives us a different plan to follow. In Matthew 5:44, it reads: "But I say unto you, *Love your enemies*, bless them that curse you, do good to them that hate you, and pray for them which despitefully use you and persecute you." This verse sounds like it could have been written directly to those going through a divorce, but am I supposed to love my enemy and bless someone who is cursing me?

What makes this even harder is that, in most cases, the person that has inflicted the most hurt upon us seems to show no signs of remorse for their actions. In many cases, their actions continue causing a need for our forgiveness from yesterday to be rekindled in order to cover the sins of today. Tami put it best when she stated, "It is very difficult to forgive someone who doesn't ask you for forgiveness. God can help you, but you have to be willing to accept that it's never going to be made right."

So why forgive? Because your forgiveness will be instrumental in your healing. You cannot look with anticipation toward the future if you are living in the past. "I let [my ex-husband] off the hook," Tami proclaimed. "I had to take him off my hook and put him on God's, and let God deal with him. That was so freeing. He's not on my hook anymore."

So often we want God to heal us from the hurt and pain that we feel, but we are not willing to turn loose of it and allow Him to do so. If you are focused on the past, you will find hurt. When you begin to look toward the future, you will find hope.

King David's journey begins

When we left King David at the end of chapter 8, he was weeping over the loss of his son Absalom. Even though Absalom had rejected and turned against his father, David still felt the pain over this loss. As word began to spread among the people that King David was grieving for his son, the "joy of the day's victory turned into deep sadness."[31]

One of David's mighty warriors, Joab, heard about David's mourning for Absalom. We pick up the story in 2 Samuel 19:5 (NLT).

> Then Joab went to the king's room and said to him, "We saved your life today and the lives of your sons, your daughters, and your wives and concubines. Yet you act like this, making us feel

---

[31] 2 Samuel 19:2

ashamed of ourselves. You seem to love those who hate you and hate those who love you. You have made it clear today that your commanders and troops mean nothing to you. It seems that if Absalom had lived and all of us had died, you would be pleased. Now go out there and congratulate your troops, for I swear by the Lord that if you don't go out, not a single one of them will remain here tonight. Then you will be worse off than ever before."

This story is given extra meaning when you realize that, after a battle, the king would traditionally go out, meet the troops, and thank them as they returned. This built morale among the troops and rapport with the king. David choosing to be alone in his mourning, rather than thanking the troops, was not only damaging to David but also demoralizing to his army.

King David chose to heed the words of Joab in verse 8: "So the king went out and took his seat at the town gate, and as the news spread throughout the town that he was there, everyone went to him." Although David had just lost his son, he, at the prodding of Joab, made himself available to the people. This action of David took his mind off of himself, and it brought hope to his army.

Peter versus Judas

On the night of Jesus's arrest, the Bible records two great betrayals of Jesus. The first is that of Judas who went to the leading priest and agreed to betray Jesus for thirty pieces of silver.[32] The other betrayal was not planned out but came in the form of a denial. Peter, after vowing that he would never deny Jesus just a few hours before, denied Jesus three times claiming that he "did not know the man."[33]

---

[32] Matthew 26:14–17
[33] Matthew 26:31–35, 69–75

Both men felt great remorse for that which they had done, but their stories go in opposite directions after this point. Judas gave up all hope and went out and hanged himself.[34] He ended his life, and thus ended any chance for redemption.

The Bible tells us, as Jesus hung on the cross, "Jesus' friends, including the women who had followed him from Galilee, stood at a distance watching" (Luke 23:49 NLT). I have to imagine that Peter was one of those friends standing at a distance and watching as Jesus was crucified. Hearing Jesus cry, "It is finished"[35] and then watching Him bow His head and die must have caused Peter to lose all hope. The guilt and shame Peter felt those next couple of days must have been overwhelming. The darkness surrounding Peter would have been crushing.

For some of you reading this right now, you feel what Peter was feeling. Not because you denied Jesus, but rather because your life has lost all hope. You may be dealing with guilt and shame. You can feel a darkness around you so dense and real that you feel as if you could reach out and touch it. You think that life will never be worth living again. You may have even considered ending it all, like Judas.

If Peter's story were to end here, it would be a sad tale like that of Judas, but that's not the end of Peter's story. On Sunday morning, Mary Magdalene, Joanna, Mary the mother of James, and several other women went to the tomb. When they arrived, they found the stone rolled away and Jesus gone. Then they saw an angel that said in verse 6, "Don't be alarmed. You are looking for Jesus of Nazareth, who was crucified. He isn't here! He is risen from the dead! Look, this is where they laid his body." Then the angel gave the most amazing instructions. Verse 7: "Now go and tell [Jesus's] disciples, *including Peter*, that Jesus is going ahead of you to Galilee."[36]

Why did the angel single out Peter? Maybe, like King David grieving the loss of his son, Peter was in a room alone grieving the loss of his friend and Savior. I think it goes deeper than that. I believe

---

[34] Matthew 27:3–5
[35] John 19:30
[36] Mark 16:4–7

it's because Jesus wanted to make sure that Peter, the one that had denied Him; Peter, the one that had wept bitterly; Peter, the one that had lost all hope; knew that he was forgiven and that hope had returned in the form of his risen Savior Jesus Christ.

The ladies quickly made their way back to where the men were and told them what had happened (Luke 24:11–12). "But the story sounded like nonsense to the men, so they didn't believe it. However, Peter jumped up and ran to the tomb to look." The other men tried to tell the ladies that they were just imagining things, but Peter, who had been sitting around in hopeless shame for three days, saw a little glimmer of hope. Peter saw that little bit of green come up from the ground. Peter saw that just maybe he would have a chance of redemption. Was Peter doubtful of their story? Possibly, but Peter saw that little green leaf sprout from the soil. Once again, Peter felt hope. He wasn't going to miss his chance to see Jesus. "Peter jumped up and ran to the tomb to look."

Like in the story of Peter, I can assure you that there is hope. You may not be able to see it at the moment, but it's there. Look closely at that little seed in the dirt. It may not happen today, and it may not happen tomorrow; but if you do your part, the day will soon come when that seed of hope will begin to produce a little leaf, then a stem, and then a rose, and eventually a beautiful bush filled with roses. You will find hope, and that hope will lead you down the path of healing.

Conclusion

Over time, it's easy to look back at the path you have traveled and see the progress made. However, it's much harder to look at the path ahead and see past the difficult obstacles in your way. The day will come, though, when you will again experience the good things in life. "When there was no pain, I took joy in other things," Susan remembered. "There is rejuvenating power in living." There is joy in your future. There is abundant life yet to be lived. Take heart. Healing has begun. There is hope.

Psalm 23 (New Life Version): The Lord—Our Shepherd

The Lord is my Shepherd. I will have everything I need.

He lets me rest in fields of green grass. He leads me beside the quiet waters.

He makes me strong again. He leads me in the way of living right with Himself which brings honor to His name.

Yes, even if I walk through the valley of the shadow of death, I will not be afraid of anything because You are with me. You have a walking stick with which to guide and one with which to help. These comfort me.

You are making a table of food ready for me in front of those who hate me. You have poured oil on my head. I have everything I need.

For sure, You will give me goodness and loving-kindness all the days of my life. Then I will live with You in Your house forever.

The Importance of Healing

> Broken people break other people, and they
> cannot have a healthy relationship.
>
> —Alissa

> You have to make some choices to
> let yourself become okay.
>
> —Tami

> *He led me to a place of safety; He rescued*
> *me because He delights in me.*
>
> —2 Samuel 22:20 NLT

Tami's story

After Tami's divorce, she sought help and comfort through Divorce Care. Divorce Care is a program specifically designed to help those going through a divorce by offering help in healing from a Christian perspective.[37] One of the first times she went to the group, she heard a couple of ladies tell their stories. "They just sobbed and sobbed," Tami recalled. "I just felt so bad for them." Tami finally asked, "How long have you been divorced?" They each answered "eight years."

---

[37] https://www.divorcecare.org

Tami was shocked. How could someone be divorced eight years and still have such raw emotions while telling their story? It was because they had never properly dealt with the feelings and effects of their divorce until then. Tami realized, "You can stay right back there forever, just trapped." These ladies had gone through all the stages of grief during their divorces, but then they "backed back up again and got trapped," Tami said. "I just determined that wasn't going to be me."

The importance of healing

Healing is such an easy word to throw out there, but why is it so important? After all, doesn't healing come with time? Steven King is credited with saying, "Time heals all wounds," but to what extent are those wounds really healed? The human body has an amazing ability to heal itself. Cuts, bruises, and even broken bones will be healed over time, but what happens if that broken bone is not set properly or if that cut is not bandaged correctly? The bone may heal, but it will not work as before if it heals in the wrong spot. Skin may regrow over that cut, but infection can develop within that wound causing a greater problem than before.

Like the body, the mind has some ability to heal itself, but if that healing only takes place due to the passage of time, the mind has not healed; it has simply filed hurts, pains, and emotions away, waiting for the next reminder to come along causing that file to be opened, the memories to be spilled out, and the scab to be ripped off the wound once again. Healing doesn't happen through avoidance; it happens through a proactive effort of meeting those hurts, pains, and emotions head-on, acknowledging them, experiencing them, dealing with them, and then filing them away.

So why is it so important to heal? Alissa noted, "Broken people break other people and cannot have a healthy relationship." Our world today, including the church world, is filled with broken people who have never healed from wounds caused by a divorce, loss of a loved one, or some other traumatic event in their lives. For some, that brokenness has led to bitterness. Others have allowed their brokenness to trap them in an introspective world where their thoughts and actions are dominated by what they need to do or get in order to find happiness again. All the time, our relationships with others and our relationship with God suffers because we are broken inside and are focused on ourselves, rather than others around us.

While walking the difficult path of divorce, it is easy to rationalize that your hurt, pain, and brokenness would just go away if you could find someone new to fill the void of your former spouse. All too often we begin looking to others as our chance to fix our problems and take away our pains. If I could just find someone else, we think, it would get my mind off my former spouse. For many, they find that other person, and their pain is masked; but their healing is put on hold. Sixty-seven percent of the time, that second marriage leads to divorce while 74 percent of third marriages fall apart.[38]

"When you go into a relationship, you have to come in healthy and be able to be an individual as well as be in the relationship," stated Alissa. "You have to be able to stand alone because, if you are so dependent on that other person for your happiness and for your well-being and to fulfill your loneliness, you will never have that fulfilled." Healing, regardless of how long it takes, is of utmost importance before you move on. Your future will only be bright after you have properly dealt with the pain from your past.

King David is welcomed back

The Bible doesn't tell us how much time elapsed between David sitting at the city gate greeting the people in 2 Samuel 19:8 and verse 11, but it is thought that weeks and probably months have passed. In verse 11, we see King David send a message to the elders of Judah. It says:

> "Why are you the last ones to welcome back the king into his palace? For I have heard that all Israel is ready. You are my relatives, my own tribe,

---

[38] https://divorcestrategiesgroup.com/why-second-marriages-fail

> my own flesh and blood! So why are you the last ones to welcome back the king?"
> And David told them to tell Amasa, "Since you are my own flesh and blood, like Joab, may God strike me and even kill me if I do not appoint you as commander of my army in his place."
> Then Amasa convinced all the men of Judah, and they responded unanimously.
> They sent word to the king, "Return to us, and bring back all who are with you." (2 Samuel 19:10–14 NLT)

David had felt the rejection of his son Absalom. He had chosen to vacate his throne and flee from his son, rather than fight. David had left Jerusalem weeping. Finally, David felt the pain of losing his son in battle. Now we see the story of David change. For close to four years, David had been fleeing Absalom and living in another country. Months, possibly up to two years, have passed since Absalom's death. The king begins his journey back to Jerusalem and ultimately back to his throne. He had endured through the most difficult time in his life and had come out victorious. It wouldn't be an easy road back to the throne, but David was now heading in the right direction.

In order to make it back to his throne in Jerusalem, David would have to overcome many obstacles. He would have to cross the Jordan River, traverse the Mount of Olives, and once again, cross the all-too-familiar Kidron Valley. He would also meet some resistance on his return trip and would have to unite the kingdom yet again. David was prepared, however, to once again become king.

Peter's healing begins

After Peter ran to the empty tomb of Jesus, he "went home again, wondering what had happened."[39] Later that day, however, Peter received his own private meeting with Jesus. Again, it is amaz-

---

[39] Luke 24:12 (NLT)

ing to realize that Jesus chose Peter as one of the first, if not the first one, to appear to. We know nothing about that meeting, except that it happened.[40] It seems that Jesus knew Peter was hurting after denying Him, and Jesus wanted Peter to know first that things were going to be okay. A few days later, we find the story recorded in John 21 (NLT) of Jesus appearing to seven of the disciples as they are fishing. They come to shore and have breakfast with Jesus on the beach. Then Jesus begins a conversation with Peter in verse 15:

> After breakfast, Jesus asked Simon, "Simon, son of John, do you love me more than these?"
> "Yes, Lord," Peter replied, "you know I love you."
> "Then feed my lambs," Jesus told him.
> Jesus repeated the question: "Simon, son of John, do you love me?"
> "Yes, Lord," Peter said, "you know I love you."
> "Then take care of my sheep," Jesus said.
> A third time, he asked him, "Simon, son of John, do you love me?"
> Peter was hurt that Jesus asked the question a third time. He said, "Lord, you know everything. You know that I love you."
> Jesus said, "Then feed my sheep."
> Three times, Jesus asks Peter, "Do you love me?" and three times Peter answers yes.

Three times Peter had denied Jesus, now three times he proclaims his love for Jesus. What we are seeing is the healing of Peter. It started with forgiveness; now Jesus is leading Peter into a deeper commitment because Jesus has great plans for Peter in the near future. However, before Peter could become the leader of the New Testament Church, he first had to overcome his shame of denying Christ. Jesus is using this opportunity on the shores of the Sea of

---

[40] Luke 24:34

Galilee to dig deep within Peter's heart and heal Peter's wound so it would never again become an obstacle for him. From that day on, Peter boldly proclaimed the name of Christ. It never would have happened, though, if Peter would have continued looking at the past and allowed his past failures to dictate his present and future.

Conclusion

So where are you today in your healing journey? As you traverse the valley of divorce, does your path look dark and bleak, or can you see daylight around the next turn? Do you spend your time looking back over the ground you have already walked, or are you looking ahead to what lies before? Maybe you are still struggling, like Peter, with your sins and mistakes of the past. Tami had to come to terms with this within her own life. She finally realized, "God can forgive us, but we have to forgive ourselves." Maybe your healing journey needs to begin with you forgiving yourself for the mistakes you made.

Healing doesn't just happen. Like Tami said, "You have to make some choices to let yourself become okay because you can stay right back there forever, just trapped." Is that where you are, trapped in your past? Tami remembers, "It was God that helped me past that." Your healing begins when you forgive yourself, forgive your spouse, and allow God to forgive you. There is light just around the next bend, but you have to leave the darkness from your past in the past. God has great plans for your life. Are you ready to look toward the future?

Psalm 23 (The Passion Translation): The Good Shepherd, David's poetic praise to God

> Yahweh is my best friend and my shepherd.
> I always have more than enough.
>
> He offers a resting place for me in His luxurious love.
> His tracks take me to an oasis of peace near
> *the quiet brook of bliss.*

That's where He restores and revives my life.
> He opens before me the right path
> and leads me along in his footsteps of righteousness
> so that I can bring honor to His name.

Even when your path takes me through
> the valley of deepest darkness,
> fear will never conquer me, for You already have!
> Your authority is my strength and my peace.
> The comfort of your love takes away my fear.
> I'll never be lonely, for You are near.

You become my delicious feast
> even when my enemies dare to fight.
> You anoint me with the fragrance of your Holy Spirit;
> You give me all I can drink of You until my cup overflows.

So why would I fear the future?
> Only goodness and tender love pursue me all the days of my life.
> Then afterward, when my life is through,
> I'll return to your glorious presence to be forever with You!

Chapter 17

Help in Healing (Friends and Family)

All of my kids really rallied around me. My parents and sisters wept for me and with me. They prayed with me.

—Don

I couldn't have made it without my family.

—Susan

The LORD also will be a refuge for the oppressed, a refuge in times of trouble.

—*Psalm 9:9 KJV*

Friends

Mark's story

As Mark's life at home was falling apart, he found that it was affecting him in the workplace. "I found myself very short-tempered and a lot more difficult to get along with. They knew something was going on, but they didn't know exactly what." This pattern continued at work until one day, things came to a head. Mark's coworkers finally said,

"Enough is enough. We've got to sit down, and you are going to have to tell us what is going on in your life." Mark began opening up to his friends at work and telling them about his struggles at home. "Those guys came around me like my wingmen," said Mark.

My (Tim's) story

Five months into my journey through the valley, one of my nearby friends came over to my house. A minor rift had occurred between us, and he came to explain why he had done what he did. After he talked for a while, I opened up and told him the loneliness and isolation that I was feeling. He was shocked.

"I see you going out, riding your bike, and fishing all the time, so I assumed you were doing okay," he said.

Doing okay? I thought.

I was doing those things because I needed to do something to keep my mind from going crazy. I explained this to him. From that day on, he made an intentional effort to walk beside me. Many evenings, after everyone else was in bed, he would come over and we would sit on my porch and talk. Most of the time, our conversations didn't revolve around my situation, but that didn't matter. He was there for me, and I knew I had a friend walking with me.

Susan's story

This close, walking-along-beside-you friendship seems to be more prevalent in women then in guys. Maybe this is because women generally are better at opening up and at listening than guys are. This was the case with Susan. She had four small groups of women from the very beginning that walked with her. Some were from her choir, some were friends from her high school days, others were from her work, and some were her close lifelong friends. "I went out with some of them every week," Susan remembers. "They saved my life. They truly did." They listened to Susan and gave her a shoulder to cry on whenever she needed it.

Two thoughts often come to mind when someone is walking through the valley of divorce. The first is, *I am the only one going through this.* The second thought is, *I don't want to bother someone else with my problems.* You may even think, *No one else cares about my struggle.* All of these thoughts are based on a false assumption, and all of them are counterproductive to one's healing.

The valley of divorce that you are experiencing is one that many others have experienced. In fact, statistics would tell us that around 40 percent[41] of marriages will end in divorce. Therefore, there are many others walking this same dark and lonely path. It is not a journey that you can or should navigate alone. Your burden will be lighter, and your healing will be quicker if you open up and allow others to walk along beside you. Don remembers his help, "Friends from church had me over for lunch or coffee. They would invite me over and just sit and visit and talk and get my mind off my heartache."

"I have a couple super-super-good friends that I could say anything to," Beth recalled. "They didn't judge me and listened whenever I was crying or yelling." Tami recalled a close friend she had during her divorce. "She was there for me," Tami said. "She just stepped in, and she would say, 'I will pick your kids up for you.'" On days that Tami had to work late, her friend would take her kids home with her until Tami could come and get them.

Each of us has a friend or friends that we are close to. Maybe, to this point, you have not opened up to that friend for any number of reasons. However, healing comes whenever we expose our wounds and ask for help. For some, this is easy to do, but for others this may be a very difficult step to take. While it may be difficult, it is important. Find that friend that can and will walk with you. It will make your journey so much easier to handle.

---

[41] https://divorcestrategiesgroup.com/why-second-marriages-fail

Family

My (Tim's) story

Seven months had passed since the day she drove away. I did my best to keep going at my current job and location. It was hard. Every moment triggered a past memory. In addition, the people I was around had only known me for a year. They had only seen me and become acquainted with me during the worst year of my life. They had watched as this drama in my life had unfolded for the world to see. I was stressed, down, and depressed. Most of them had never really seen the real me. I needed to be around people who truly knew me.

I began seeking a new beginning with a new job and new location. Weeks turned into months as I waited to receive word on a couple of possible job opportunities. Through it all, only one door opened. The day came when I made the call. "Dad," I said, "would it be okay if I moved back home for a couple of months?" It was now mid-September. My plan was to be home during the holiday season and wait there for other doors to open. At the very least, I would be home surrounded by family and friends that knew the real me. "Sure," Dad replied, and I began preparing for yet another move. Little did I realize the impact this move would have on my healing journey.

As stated before, each of the primary people interviewed for this book grew up in a good, Christian, two-parent home. While that heritage brings a stigma while going through a divorce, it also brings great stability as well. For each of us, that solid foundation that we experienced during our childhood continued during our darkest days of life. Don recalls, "All of my kids really rallied around me. My parents and sisters wept with me and prayed for me."

Mark felt this same love and support from his family, even though Mark had messed up. "I knew that my parents were disappointed in some of the choices that I had made and that I was getting a divorce," Mark said, "but they assured me that they loved me and cared about me and that they were there for me. They weren't necessarily taking my side, but they were there to love me and support me." Now Mark says, "Looking back, it meant the world to me."

Tami recalls how much her family support meant. "My dad was really there for me. He would always encourage me. He was my go-to. He just listened and listened. He was always there when I needed something. When my kids got older, I feel like they were instrumental in helping me to heal too."

My story continues

I moved back home, went back to my home church with people I had known all my life, and began working construction during the week with a longtime friend. The familiar environment, lifelong friends, and close family gave me the stability and foundation that I had longed for. My outlook on life quickly improved, and I soon began looking toward the future, rather than living in the past.

Family can provide a comfort and stability like no one else when going through difficult times. For some, however, family that should bring comfort instead brings more pain and rejection. What does one do in such a situation? How do you cope when your family support system is not very supportive? We find our answer in Psalm 27:10–11. It reads, "When my father and my mother forsake me, then the Lord will take care of me. Teach me your way, O Lord, and lead me in a smooth path because of my enemies" (NKJV).

Sometimes, family tells us things we don't want to hear. They have the ability to see things in us that we don't see or are unwilling to see. During those times, we must be honest with ourselves, look deep inside, and see if their unwelcome advice may, in fact, be wise advice. The best support comes from those who are willing to tell us what we need to hear and not just what we want to hear.

In those cases, though, where your family rejects you, you can know that there is a god who will take care of you. If you will allow Him to do so, He will lead you down the right path and will walk with you through the valley.

*Psalm 23 (Expanded Bible): The Lord
the Shepherd, A psalm of David*

> The LORD is my shepherd;
>> I have everything I need [will lack nothing].
>
> He lets me rest [makes me lie down] in green pastures.
>> He leads me to calm [quiet] water.
>
> He gives me new strength [renews my soul].
> He leads me on paths that are right [righteous *or* straight]
>> for the good [sake] of his name [reputation].
>
> Even if I walk through a very dark valley [*or* the shadow of death],
>> I will not be afraid [fear no evil],
> because you are with me.
>> Your rod and your shepherd's staff comfort me.
> You prepare a meal [table] for me
>> in front [the presence] of my enemies.
> You pour oil of blessing on my head [anoint my head with oil; oil was a means of refreshment in a hot, dry environment];
>> You fill my cup to overflowing [make my cup overflow; a cup of blessing].
>
> Surely your goodness and love [loyalty; mercy] will be with [pursue; follow] me
>> all my life,
> and I will live in the house of the LORD forever [for length of days].

Chapter 18

Our Living Hope

I couldn't make it through my life
without Him, even now.

—Tami

He was crying with me in my pain, and
He knew what I was going through.

—Susan

*In peace I will lie down and sleep, for you
alone, Lord, make me dwell in safety.*

—*Psalm 4:8 NIV*

Beth's story

It was late into the night, and Beth couldn't sleep. She was in the midst of her divorce, and her young son was gone to his father's house. As the time neared 3:00 a.m., Beth found herself aimlessly flipping through channels on the TV, trying to pass the time until she would fall asleep. She happened to stop for a moment on a channel where a preacher was preaching. As she did, the preacher said, "God cares more about healing broken hearts than condemning people for the mistakes they made."

"That made a huge impact on me," Beth recalled. "It helped me that night when I couldn't sleep."

In the first chapter of this book, we talked of how King David probably wrote Psalm 23 during his escape from Absalom. Throughout this book, Psalm 23 has been printed in many different Bible translations. We have followed the story of David and Absalom, and while the situation was different, the dark valley that David walked has many similarities to the valley of divorce. Also, the god that David followed in Psalm 23 is the same god that can lead us through life's most difficult valleys today. With this in mind, let's break down Psalm 23 and see how it applies to our lives today as we see this god who is truly our living hope.

The Lord is my Shepherd (following God)

David made it clear right away that the Lord is a personal god. He says, the Lord is MY shepherd. David could have said, "The Lord is a shepherd," and that would have been symbolically true. God leads His children along and provides and cares for them just like a shepherd leads his sheep along. However, David made it personal. David is declaring himself as one of God's sheep. He is a follower of God. Therefore, he can say with complete certainty that the Lord is his shepherd.

Tami knows this personal shepherd that David speaks of. "It was probably in the last year of my marriage that I turned it all over to God," Tami recalls. "I was actually in bed and said a simple prayer of repentance that I was never going to walk away again. [Since then] God has grown me, and chastened me, and healed me, and held me. The old songs that talk about a peace that passes all understanding, I know what that means now. I would literally just pray, and I would have a peace."

I shall not want (trusting God)

How could David proclaim, "I shall not want," shortly after vacating his throne and while escaping through the wilderness. It would seem that this would be the time that David would want and be asking for more things than ever. Maybe it is because David was finding out what many of us have discovered while going through a difficult valley. It is during these times that the Lord shows Himself, brings peace, and fills those voids that others cannot fill.

Alissa can attest to this as well. "Going through hard times, I'm so thankful that God isn't who I thought He was. He's not in that box. He's so much bigger. He's so much more compassionate. He's so much more understanding. In God's perfect will, I don't think He wants any of us to be hurt, but in His permissive will, He will allow us to go down the paths that we go and be broken. But out of that, He will use His perfect will to bring about His good. I've just learned that God is much more than my little box could ever contain. He is amazing."

He makes me to lie down in green pastures (Drawing closer to God)

Here, we see David likening himself to a sheep. It is said that sheep will not lie down until they are full, content, and feel safe. How could David feel content when he had just left his throne? How could he feel safe when he was fleeing for his life? How could he feel full when his life was in an uproar? There is only one way this could happen. David found comfort, and he found peace in knowing that he was being led by the Good Shepherd.

During Don's darkest days, he too experienced this peace that David spoke of. "I would walk through the house singing and praying. It was remarkably therapeutic to worship and to pray and to sing. I was able to sleep better at night when I started doing that. I was able to let go of the pain. Even though I was hurting, I felt like it accelerated my healing quite a bit. Scriptures came alive to me. It was an enriching experience. In spite of the pain, God was with me. It was maybe the closest time with God that I ever had in my life."

He leads me beside the still waters (The leading hand of God)

We once again see David likening himself to a sheep. Sheep will not drink out of a roaring river. No. The water must be calm and still before a sheep will get close enough to drink. Even though David found himself in a season of life where the waters were rough and scary, he still found that when he followed the Lord, his shepherd David felt calm inside of him, even though there was turmoil on the outside.

Mark had strayed away from the Lord, his shepherd, during the time of his separation and divorce. However, today, Mark can look back and see how the leading hand of God brought others into his life during this pivotal time. "I do sometimes wonder if it was His hand that was directing the people around me that were helping me. Maybe it wasn't just the friendships and the family relationship. Maybe it was God's hand in guiding them into my pathway, so maybe I can look back and say that that was God working on me even before I asked Him for help." By leading others into Mark's pathway, God began leading Mark back to Him where Mark could, once again, find the peace of the still waters.

He restores my soul (The restoring hand of God)

Here, David shows that even though his world was crashing down around him, God brought peace and restoration to David on the inside. His future looked bleak from human eyes, but since David was following God, he found inner strength during the most difficult times.

One month before my divorce was finalized, I was in Kansas City for the weekend staying with a good friend. On Sunday morning, he took me to a church that he had been attending. It was in North Kansas City, and he and I were the only White people there. After a fun and lively time of worship, the pastor got up and began to speak. For a quick forty-five minutes, he spoke with great fire and enthusiasm.

The pastor ended his sermon and began to pray a closing prayer. One sentence into his prayer, he stopped praying and said, "You on the aisle." I didn't need to look up. I knew he was speaking to me. "You are going through a very difficult time right now," he said. "God has given me a message for you. He knows that you are struggling with a broken relationship." I had never met this pastor before. He did not know me from Adam. He continued, "God is telling me to tell you to spend thirty minutes a day for the next seven days praying to Him. Ask Him to restore your relationships."

That night, as I traveled home, I began praying. As I tried to pray, I was having trouble formulating complete sentences. I realized that I didn't really know what I wanted to pray for. While I longed to have the pain and hurt of my separation and pending divorce go away, I didn't really want things to go back to how they were before. For thirty minutes, I stuttered and stammered around before God.

On night two, my prayer was about the same. By night three, I was picking up steam. I was beginning to pray for God to perform His will as I literally did not know what my will or desire even was. After night four, I still did not know what I wanted, but I was willing to let God lead the way.

The next evening, an incident happened that solidified that it was time to look forward and not back. The next morning, I woke up with a feeling of excitement for the weekend that lay ahead. I hadn't felt excitement for months. On Saturday morning, I woke up with a sweet feeling of peace. Things were changing, but they were not outward changes—they were changing within me. That weekend, I began to feel the restoring hand of God on my soul. While my marital status did not change, my relationship with God did. Subsequently, many old and new relationships with many others began to grow stronger, and with each strengthened or new relationship, God renewed my soul a little more. Through it all, God is restoring my soul.

He leads me in paths of righteousness for His name's sake (The strong hand of God)

David continues by proclaiming God's goodness by leading him in paths of righteousness. When David followed God, the path was not always easy, but it was always good because he was following the Good Shepherd. Why does God do this? Simply to show His goodness to us. Through following God, we begin to find our self-worth, not in others but in Him.

Tami feels this same longing to follow after God as He leads. "I don't seem to be able to reach a stage where I feel that I am able to do for God. He always has to do for me. He continually has to pick me up and strengthen me to get going. I'm just weak and frail. However, He continues to help me. It's not a sinful kind of weakness but rather a frailness of the human and a weakness of emotion. I have to spend more time praying for myself and less time praying for others." God continues to lead Tami down the right path. Why? Because she continues to follow Him, and in her weakness, God shows Himself to be more than enough.

Even though I walk through the valley of the shadow of death, I will fear no evil (The God of comfort)

As David penned these words, they had more meaning than ever. Ever since David was a young boy, he knew about the Kidron Valley, also known as the valley of the shadow of death. He had undoubtedly walked this valley many times on the short journey between his hometown of Bethlehem and Jerusalem. He had probably been fearful as he walked through the massive graveyard shortly before entering the eastern gate of Jerusalem. However, on this day, while walking across the valley of the shadow of death, it had even more meaning for David. His life was in danger as his own son Absalom sought to kill him. He had every reason to fear evil and fear death, but David proclaimed, because he was following the Good Shepherd, he would fear no evil even while in the valley of the shadow of death.

Susan found this to be true in her own life as she walked through dark times. "God firmly brought scriptures to mind. He brought songs to my mind. I remember sitting in some services, going, 'Thank you [Lord] that was for me.' Sometimes, it was almost so divine that I knew God was crying with me in my pain and what I was going through. He knew." This same god that walked with David across the "valley of the shadow of death" and over the Mount of Olives came alongside Susan and walked with her as she walked through the valley of divorce.

Thy rod and thy staff, they comfort me (Giving God control)

David had a great understanding of not only the leading hand of God but also the correcting, guiding, and protecting hand of God. The shepherd's rod was used to guide the sheep while sometimes pulling them back on the path if they started to wander off. David did not fight this correction but rather was thankful for it. That same instrument of correction could also be used as an instrument of protection against whatever might come to harm the sheep. Again, David was comforted in knowing that his Lord would protect him from all evil that tried to overtake him.

Mark recalls in his own life when he finally stepped back and allowed God to lead and correct him. "There was a point in time where I realized that my failures and my shortcomings had led to this point in my life. I said, 'God, I need you to step back in and help me and direct me.' It wasn't until after that occurred that more positive things began to happen in my life with relationships."

Conclusion

Through the first four verses of Psalm 23, we can see the special relationship that David had with his Lord and Savior. It was through this relationship that David was able to trust God and find peace even during the difficult journey out of Jerusalem. While David would need time to heal, he expressed hope even in the middle of possibly his darkest day.

This hope that David expressed is the same hope that others in this book have shown. Although like any hope, it has to be grounded in something true and real. This hope is based on a god that not only walks beside us in difficult times but willingly gave up His life for us so we could walk with Him.

While you should lean on family and friends during this difficult journey, complete healing will only happen when you lay your burdens at the foot of the cross of Jesus. Others can bring us comfort, but only Jesus can provide true healing. He will not only walk with you through the valley, but He will also bring you out on the other side. He truly is our living hope.

Psalm 23 (New International Version): A psalm of David

The Lord is my shepherd, I lack nothing.

He makes me lie down in green pastures; He leads me beside quiet waters,

He refreshes my soul. He guides me along the right paths for His name's sake.

Even though I walk through the darkest valley, I will fear no evil, for You are with me; your rod and your staff, they comfort me.

You prepare a table before me in the presence of my enemies.

You anoint my head with oil; my cup overflows.

Surely your goodness and love will follow me all the days of my life, and I will dwell in the house of the Lord forever.

SECTION 6

Coming Alive

It makes you realize that you can go through great, deep sorrow and you can come out of it. It's like, now what do you have to throw at me, life? I've been at the bottom. You can't touch me.

—Susan

*Therefore, if anyone is in Christ,
the new creation has come:
The old has gone, the new is here!*

—*2 Corinthians 5:17 NLT*

Coming alive

As that seed of healing begins to sprout and grow, something wonderful begins to happen within you. Your focus begins to change. You are no longer looking at your past. Instead, you begin anticipating your future. Excitement and energy that have long been dormant begin to reemerge. You realize that you are again experiencing hopes and dreams. Things you used to enjoy before your divorce once more sound fun.

Your goals begin to change from daily goals, like "I have to get some exercise today," or "I've got to start dinner," or "I must do some cleaning around the house," to future goals, like "I would like to run a 5K," or "I should have a big backyard barbeque with a bunch of friends," or "I would love to remodel the kitchen or bathroom." You may not even realize the subtle change at first, but over time, you can see that something is different.

Your thoughts are no longer a game plan of how you will navigate and survive the day, but rather a plan of how you will start that new project or save for that vacation with the kids or plan that big party or celebration. Yes, something is different, but it is not necessarily your situation. As the scars from your past begin to scab over and heal, you are left with more hope and energy that can be focused toward the future. Your situation may still be the same, but your perspective is different.

Make no mistake. Many wounds leave scars even after they heal. Evidence of the wound will always be visible even though it doesn't hurt like it did the first time that dagger pierced through your flesh, leaving a gaping hole in your innermost being. Pictures, events, places, people, and any host of other things will trigger painful thoughts and memories of the difficult journey you have traveled. However, as you peer into the future, you now see hope instead of despair. Behind you are the graves of broken promises, shattered dreams, betrayal, rejection, and so much more. In front of you, though, lies new opportunities, new dreams, new experiences, and new memories waiting to be made. They have always been there, but it was not until now that they have come into focus.

As you look ahead, one more thing catches your eye. The walls of this deep, dark valley are getting smaller. For the first time, you catch a glimpse of what you have longed to see for months or even years. With each step, your valley is being replaced by a beautiful open plain filled with a wonderful world of endless opportunities. That seed has turned into a beautiful rose bush. There is only one way to explain this change that has happened within you. You are finally coming alive!

Chapter 19

Loving Yourself

> I was busy, and maybe for the first time in my life, finding out who I really was down deep inside.
>
> —Mark

> I don't believe that anybody else can truly love you if you don't love yourself.
>
> —Alissa

> *Keep me as the apple of Your eye; hide me under the shadow of Your wings.*
>
> —*Psalm 17:8 NKJV*

Don's story

After his wife left, Don began going to a therapist. The therapist soon realized that Don had lost his own identity. His identity was totally wrapped up in being known as his wife's husband, and being his kids' father, and in his position at work. Don didn't really know who he was. One day, his therapist gave him an assignment. Don was to write a letter to himself about himself. He was to write about different things that he liked and loved about himself. "It was really hard to do," Don recalled, "because we are not used to thinking in terms of 'I really love myself' or 'I'm a great guy.' It helped me to identify some really good things about me and the things I really liked about myself. Being able to do that was a game changer for me," said Don. "I felt like I could now be my own person. I did not have to be [her] husband. I could be me."

Loving oneself

Possibly more so than about any other event in life, a divorce can wreck a person's confidence and self-image. When the one person that took a vow to love and cherish you chooses instead to walk out on you, the shock waves can be devastating. If the person that knows you best finds you unworthy of their love, what does that say about you? *If my spouse doesn't love me*, we think, *I must be unlovable.*

The truth, however, is that your spouse isn't the one person that knows you best. You are the one that knows you like no other. You know your deepest secrets and struggles. You know your insecurities and your strengths. You know your past mistakes and your future goals. So the question must be asked, Do you love you? Better yet, Do you like you? What do you think when you see that person staring back at you in the mirror? You see, how you perceive yourself will go a long way in determining how others will view you.

"Learning to love myself has been big," said Alissa. "I have made myself look in the mirror a lot and remind myself that God made me. I don't believe that anybody else can truly love you if you don't love yourself." This has been a daily process for Alissa. She is not only working to love herself but also working to better those areas about herself that she doesn't like. "I want to be able to be confident in who I am in my own frame, in my own body, in my own mind, and comfortable in my own skin before I expect anyone else to love me in the way that I desire to be loved." Like Don, Alissa is actively learning to love the person she has become.

For some, the hardest obstacle to overcome in a divorce is forgiving themselves. "God can forgive us, but we have to forgive ourselves," stated Tami. This is something that Beth experienced as well. "Over time," said Beth, "I began to forgive myself." It is in forgiving ourselves that we begin to heal and are able to come alive.

Susan recalls those early days after her separation and divorce. "I sold the house I was in and moved into a little apartment and made it totally my own. I bought a car. I had never bought a car before. I worked myself out of debt." Susan eventually bought a house. Her independence built her confidence, or maybe her confidence helped to build her independence. Either way, Susan began to realize that she had the ability to not only survive but to thrive on her own.

You are loved

So how do you learn to love yourself? It begins with the realization that you are loved by the One that knows you best. We stated earlier that your spouse is not the one that knows you best. However, neither are you. You are best known not by man but rather by your Creator. In Psalm 139:14, the psalmist writes, "I praise you [God] because I am fearfully and wonderfully made; your works are wonderful, I know that full well" (NIV).

You are not a clump of cells that kept multiplying until one day, you randomly became a fetus and eventually a newborn. You are not just another human without a purpose, inhabiting the earth until one day you die. If that is your view of yourself, you will never have confidence or love for who you are.

The truth is this—you were "fearfully and wonderfully made" by a god who loves you so much that He sent His Son to die for you, so you can spend eternity with Him after you die.[42] You were pieced together in your mother's womb[43] for a special purpose. God has special plans for your life. Those plans are "plans to prosper you and not to harm you, plans to give you hope and a future" (Jeremiah 29:11b NIV). What has happened in your life is not the end of the story. It is only one chapter. The rest of your story is yet to be written, and the one that knows you better than anyone else loves you more than anyone else; and He wants to make something beautiful out of the next chapter of your life.

---

[42] John 3:16
[43] Psalm 139:13

When you learn to view yourself through the lens of your Creator, you will begin seeing yourself the way that He sees you. He will forgive you for your past, but you have to forgive yourself as well. Why does it matter? Because you're about to begin writing the next chapter of your story. When you learn to love yourself with all your imperfections, you will begin to come alive. When that happens, the overflow of what is within you will cause you to view others in a whole new light. Most of all, the joy and confidence that you begin to show will cause others to view you differently as well. You are coming alive, and people are about to experience the new you.

Psalm 23 (Tree of Life Version): A<small>DONAI</small>*-Ro-eh*

A psalm of David. A<small>DONAI</small> is my shepherd, I shall not want.

He makes me lie down in green pastures. He leads me beside still waters.

He restores my soul. He guides me in paths of righteousness for His name's sake.

Even though I walk through the valley of the shadow of death, I will fear no evil for You are with me: your rod and your staff comfort me.

You prepare a table before me in the presence of my enemies.

You have anointed my head with oil, my cup overflows.

Surely, goodness and mercy will follow me all the days of my life, and I will dwell in the House of A<small>DONAI</small> forever.

Chapter 20

Loving Others

> I feel like, in some ways, God has given me
> His eyes because of the last ten years.
>
> —Alissa

> Part of your healing will be in being able to
> sit down with someone and say, "Here's what
> happened to me and let me encourage you."
>
> —Susan

> *Bear one another's burdens, and so*
> *fulfill the law of Christ.*
>
> —*Psalm 17:8 NKJV*

Alissa's story

"I've always loved people, but now I see people," said Alissa. If you have walked through the dark valley of divorce or the death of a spouse, you will begin to understand this statement. Alissa understands this all too well. "I do not regret the last ten years. That is very healing for me because I see where it brought me and how it changed me," Alissa remarked, "and when I see a homeless person or a drugged-out person, I see my ex-husband. I see his family; I see people with holes. Now when people tell me about the horrible people in their lives, I hurt for them."

Alissa continued, "When I see people now, I don't just see their ugliness or their sin. I see them, and I know that something in them is so broken and now they break other people. That's what broken people do. They sabotage the good. They sabotage the people who love them the most. [My experience] changed my viewpoint of people. It gave me a compassion."

As Alissa began to cry, she noted, "I feel like, in some ways, God has given me His eyes because of the last ten years. Because of being broken I began to see people, and they want love. They just think that love is a needle, or the next bed, or getting people to feel a certain way about them. They don't realize that [God] is love. I am thankful for the last ten years. Everything we walk through, if we turn it over to God, He will use it. I want to love people where they are. I want to love them as they sit here and weep. [God] has given me such a love for people, and for that I am eternally grateful."

For someone who has not experienced the deep valley or the healing touch of God, these words may sound like a foreign language. How could someone love another person who has wronged them or others? When I was younger, I discovered something fascinating. I would go into a dark room, wait a few seconds, and then shine a flashlight into my eye while looking in the mirror. After being in the dark for a few seconds, my pupil would expand in order to allow more light into my eye. We all learned this in school. When I shone the flashlight into my eye, I could watch in the mirror as my greatly expanded pupil quickly reduced down to a small black dot.

In a spiritual sense, the same thing happens when one walks through a dark valley. As we go through a difficult time, God often opens our eyes wider, and we begin to see others like He sees them. We stop simply looking at their actions and begin to look at the why behind such actions.

Often, as our eyes are opened wider, our heart begins to open up as well. We hurt with those who hurt because we can empathize with them. We see their actions as a response to their pain, rather than an indicator of who they truly are. We also begin to see the struggles and needs of others around us more clearly.

Loving others that are divorced

Opened eyes and a loving heart may be most noticeable to a divorced person when they hear about someone else who is now starting down into the dark valley of divorce. "My attitude has changed toward the person who is suffering through a divorce," stated Don. "My perspective is changed. I'm a lot softer and much less judgmental. I see it as a sign of brokenness."

Mark has a similar story. "I know that going through this process and being a divorced individual has suddenly made me stop and realize that judging others, first of all, is not healthy for them. Second, it's not healthy for me. I've learned to accept people with way more latitude than I did when I was younger."

So often, our first reaction when we hear of a divorce is to attempt to assign fault. Susan related to this. "I used to think when people were divorced, who's fault is it? I never do that now." Someone observing from a distance will never know the whole story. However, for those who have walked through the valley, they understand the pain and know the journey. This common bond leads to a more open heart and mind toward one going through a separation and divorce.

Loving others that have wronged you

To love someone from a distance that is hurting like you hurt is noble. However, how do you love someone when you are the one they hurt? It is much easier to love the person holding a dagger when the dagger is not facing your direction. It is much easier to forgive their unkind words and actions when those words and actions are directed at someone else. It is much easier to look past the what and look at the why when it doesn't directly harm you.

Thou preparest a table before me in the presence of mine enemies (looking past our enemies)

In Chapter 18, we looked at the first four verses of Psalm 23. Now let's continue by looking at the first part of verse 5, "Thou preparest a table before me in the presence of mine enemies." King David knew the feeling of the dagger piercing his soul as his son Absalom rebelled against him. David also knew the necessity of "watching his back" for fear for his life. Yet at the beginning of verse 5, David paints a rather unusual picture. It is a visual of one sitting down to enjoy a meal while surrounded on the battlefield by those who would choose to destroy him. It is not a picture of turmoil and chaos, however, but rather a picture of peace even in the presence of his enemies. Further, the verse lays out a picture of great joy, met needs, and fellowship while his enemies look on, unable to do anything to harm him or disrupt the occasion.

So often we look with contempt at the one who hurt us when instead we should be looking toward God, the One who will help and heal us. The first step toward finding love for your enemy is to find peace with God. For Don, the first step was when a friend told him, "God knew on your wedding day that she was going to walk away from you."

"The fact that He knew that, but He's still there," said Don, "and His hand is still working in my life, and being able to realize that He is not done with me, that is a tremendous encouragement. A tremendous comfort."

What Don is conveying is the healing step of looking toward Jesus and trusting in Him, rather than looking back. Knowing this is not his story but simply a chapter gives Don the will to keep going. Don says that he can now "transmit that to other people and let them know that God is not done with them either."

King David's mercy to Shimei

As King David crossed the Jordan River on his way back to the throne in Jerusalem, we see an interesting story play out. Shimei ran out to meet David and help him across. That name may sound familiar. We talked about Shimei in chapter 3. He was the one who, as David fled Jerusalem, over the Mount of Olives, threw rocks and dirt at David and cursed him. On David's darkest day, Shimei was there doing all he could to disgrace David and hurt him.

This day was different. David was returning triumphantly to his throne. Who should appear? Shimei. This time, his demeanor is different. Shimei knows that David could kill him on the spot. We pick up the story in verse 18.

> As the king was about to cross the river, Shimei fell down before him.
>
> "My lord the king, please forgive me," he pleaded. "Forget the terrible thing your servant did when you left Jerusalem. May the king put it out of his mind. I know how much I sinned. That is why I have come here today, the very first person in all Israel to greet my lord the king."
>
> Then Abishai, son of Zeruiah, said, "Shimei should die for he cursed the LORD's anointed king!"
>
> "Who asked your opinion, you sons of Zeruiah!" David exclaimed. "Why have you become my adversary today? This is not a day for execution, for today I am once again the king of Israel!" Then turning to Shimei, David vowed, "Your life will be spared." (2 Samuel 19:18–23 NLT)

This could have been David's revenge tour. All those who had betrayed him could have died for their crimes. Yet David takes a different approach. David forgave Shimei and spared his life. Why? Maybe it was because David had experienced God's forgiveness when David had sinned with Bathsheba. Or maybe it was because David had just walked through the longest, darkest, and deepest valley of his life, and God had opened his eyes and heart where he now saw Shimei not for what he had done, but he saw him through the eyes of God.

Father, forgive them

The forgiveness of David is amazing, but it pales to compare to the forgiveness that Christ demonstrated. After Christ had been rejected, beaten, mocked, tortured, lied about, and stripped naked, his accusers nailed Him to a cross and hung His battered body for all to see. As Jesus hung on the cross, fighting for breath, He looked toward God in heaven and said, "Father, forgive them, for they do not know what they do" (Luke 23:34a). How could Christ make such a request for those who had abused and crucified Him? He looked past the who and saw their hearts that were in need of forgiveness and in need of a Savior. He understood that they did not know what they were doing. He forgave them even though they had no remorse and did not ask for forgiveness. Through it all, He loved them.

Conclusion

Maybe David is referred to as "a man after God's own heart" in the Bible because of his ability to look through people and forgive them like Jesus did while on the cross. However, David is not the only one who is expected to forgive. Ephesians 4:32 says, "And be kind to one another, tenderhearted, forgiving one another, even as God in Christ forgave you" (NKJV). God expects us to love and forgive others too. After all, that is what He did for us.

While the valley you are in may seem deep and dark, it will also open your eyes if you allow it to do so. "I think it's made me a kinder and more loving person. I have no stones to throw," stated Tami. Your walk through the valley will change you, but that change can be positive. You will begin to see others who are broken, and you will feel their pain. Why? Because it is much easier to see broken people once you've been broken. It is after this that you truly learn the joy and blessing in loving others.

Psalm 23 (Young's Literal Translation)

> A Psalm of David, Jehovah [is] my shepherd, I do not lack,
> In pastures of tender grass, He causeth me to lie down. By quiet waters, He doth lead me.
> My soul He refresheth. He leadeth me in paths of righteousness, for His name's sake,

Also when I walk in a valley of death-shade, I fear no evil, for Thou [art] with me. Thy rod and Thy staff—they comfort me.

Thou arrangest before me a table, over-against my adversaries, Thou hast anointed with oil my head. My cup is full!

Only goodness and kindness pursue me, all the days of my life, and my dwelling [is] in the house of Jehovah, for a length of days!

Chapter 21

Loving God

He was so personal in such a personal pain.

—Susan

He cares and listens, and He sends
both big and small blessings.

—Beth

*Draw near to God and He will draw near
to you. Cleanse your hands, you sinners; and
purify your hearts, you double-minded.*

—*James 4:8 NKJV*

Alissa's story

As Alissa sat and pondered, she recalled memories from her childhood of her heroes of the faith. "They would get up during church and weep. They would wave their hankies and say, 'Oh, the faithfulness of God!' I remember them just shouting. I remember looking at them and thinking, *I want to feel that.*" Alissa said, "As they told their story you could see the conviction and the power in them as they would weep and talk about what God has brought them through, and I wanted it. And I got it! But it came at a price."

At the beginning of the journey, few, if any, would willingly go through the valley if there were any way to avoid it. However, many of those who have traveled down that dark road will report that during their journey, they experienced God in a way that they never had before. "He was so personal, in such a personal pain," reported Susan. "He just brought so many things, so many people, and sermons to let me know that this is a god who cares about every little nuance in [my] life."

Thou anointest my head with oil (healing the hurts and scars)

As David continued to pen the words of Psalm 23, he wrote the sentence, "Thou anointest my head with oil." At first, this sentence may bring confusion as we read it. However, when you look at it through the eyes of David as a shepherd first and then a king, you begin to see the beauty in these words.

In his book, *A Shepherd Looks at Psalm 23*, W. Phillip Keller speaks of the knowledge he gained during his years as a shepherd. Keller tells of how summer flies would torment the sheep. In some cases, flies would fly up into the nasal cavity of the sheep and lay their eggs. The sheep would get so distressed at this discomfort that they would begin beating their head against a rock or tree, sometimes causing injury or even death.

The shepherd, knowing the discomfort the flies brought to his sheep, would put a homemade oil on the sheep and on the nasal cavity. This anointing with oil caused the flies to stay away and brought comfort and peace to the sheep[44] (Keller 138–140).

As the days of summer passed and fall began, so did mating season for the sheep. The rams went to war with each other over the ewes. In their fighting, two rams would often smash their horns together. This tremendous impact could again hurt or even kill the ram. A loving shepherd once again placed oil on the horns of the rams. This oil, however, was a thick oil or grease. When the rams tried to attack each other, the oil eliminated friction, causing the

---

[44] W. Phillip Keller, *A Shepherd Looks at Psalm 23*. Zondervan, 2007.

rams' horns to slide off the horns of its opponent. The lack of a direct impact greatly reduced the possibility of serious injury or death[45] (Keller 146–147).

David, being a shepherd, would have been familiar with both of these practices and their results. David also, however, knew what it was like to be anointed. In 1 Samuel 16, we find the story of the Prophet Samuel coming to the house of Jessie. God had led Samuel there and told him that he was to anoint one of Jessie's sons as the future king of Israel. After looking at all of the sons that Jessie brought forward, Samuel asked (verse 11), "Are these all the sons you have?"

"There is still the youngest," Jesse replied. "But he's out in the fields watching the sheep and goats."

"Send for him at once," Samuel said. "We will not sit down to eat until he arrives."

So Jesse sent for him. He was dark and handsome with beautiful eyes.

And the LORD said, "This is the one. Anoint him."

So as David stood there among his brothers, Samuel took the flask of olive oil he had brought and anointed David with the oil. And the Spirit of the LORD came powerfully upon David from that day on. Then Samuel returned to Ramah" (NLT).

Yes, David knew what it was like to anoint sheep, but he also knew what it was like to be anointed by God. In this verse, however, we see David comparing God to the shepherd and pouring out His anointing oil on us. Why? To protect us from the little "flies" that plague us day after day, minute after minute, and can cause us to suffer great torment. There are also times when God brings out the big can of axle grease and rubs it on us to protect us from others who would challenge us or to protect us from hurting ourselves when we charge into a situation that we should have avoided.

When you are walking through the valley of divorce, those flies may be memories or experiences that plague you day after day. The what ifs and broken dreams can be crushing as they continue to pester your mind, causing you to be trapped in the prison of your own

---

[45] W. Phillip Keller, *A Shepherd Looks at Psalm 23*. Zondervan, 2007.

thoughts. Maybe those flies are harsh, hate filled, or untrue words that have been said to you or about you. Can you ever get them out of your mind? While some of these things may never completely disappear, the gentle, soothing effect of the anointing oil of God on our minds can bring about peace. Even though the flies may swarm around us, they cannot harm us.

Maybe your battle is ongoing as you and your ex continue to butt heads over the children, the house, money, or any number of other things. For you, the anointing of God may be needed in order to make your words less cutting, your tone softer, and your response guarded. The oil is needed to remove friction and bring resolution and comfort in your life and in your current situation.

My story

As I walked through the difficult times leading up to my separation and ultimate divorce, a couple of close friends would tell me, "Get closer to God." I would dutifully smile and nod. I was a Christian. I was serving God. Even my job was a ministry.

My problem wasn't my relationship with God, I thought, *but rather my relationship with my spouse.*

The day came, however, when I began actively seeking God and drawing closer to Him. (I spoke of this in chapter 18.) When I began drawing closer to God, things began changing in my life. At first, those changes were internal. My perspective began to change. Hope began to spring forth. I began looking toward the future with anticipation.

Those internal changes soon turned external. I began writing about my story, and others began contacting me and confiding in me. My eyes were opened to the hurts and needs of others. My relationships with so many others began to grow and flourish. Speaking opportunities emerged. Lastly, job opportunities in ministry opened up. My world changed for the better. However, my outside world changed after my inside world changed. I first began to see and know God more intimately, and then I began to see and know others through His eyes.

Conclusion

It is through the most difficult journeys of life that we really begin to learn who God truly is. "God can take even the most broken life and turn it around and do something beautiful with it," stated Mark, "and that's what happened with me." Perhaps Alissa put it best when she said, "I am so thankful that God isn't who I thought He was. He's not in that box. He is so much bigger. He is so much more compassionate. He is so much more understanding." That is who God is and to know Him is to love Him. When you love God, your world within and the world you see around you will never look the same again. Loving yourself and loving others only truly begins by first loving God.

Psalm 23 (The Voice)

> The Eternal is my shepherd; He cares for me always.
> He provides me rest in rich, green fields
> > beside streams of refreshing water.
> > *He soothes my fears;*
> He makes me whole again,
> > steering me *off worn, hard paths*
> > to roads where *truth and* righteousness echo
> > His name.
> Even in the *unending* shadows of death's darkness,
> > I am not overcome by fear.
> Because You are with me *in those dark moments,*
> > near with your protection and guidance,
> > I am comforted.
> You spread out a table before me,
> > *provisions* in the midst of *attack from* my enemies;
> You *care for all my needs,* anointing my head with *soothing, fragrant* oil,
> > filling my cup again and again *with your grace.*

Certainly your faithful protection and loving provision will pursue me
    where I go, always, everywhere.
I will always be with the Eternal,
    in your house forever.

Chapter 22

Living Life

> You can't really think about the future
> when you are going through a divorce.
> Now I can be more forward thinking.
>
> —Don

> I have dreams again.
>
> —Beth

> *To all who mourn in Israel, He will*
> *give a crown of beauty for ashes,*
> *a joyous blessing instead of mourning,*
> *festive praise instead of despair.*
> *In their righteousness, they will be like great oaks*
> *that the LORD has planted for His own glory.*
>
> —*James 4:8 NLT*

Tami's story

After Tami's divorce, she looked for something that would bring fulfillment again. During this time, the pianists at Tami's church moved. The pastor came to Tami and asked if she would be the church pianist. This was a big decision for her. She did not feel comfortable playing the piano, especially in front of a crowd.

"Would you feel better if we had a guitar?" asked the pastor.

"Yes, that would help," responded Tami.

Along came a drummer to join them, and they had a worship team.

"The things that helped me move forward," remembered Tami, "was being active and involving myself in things, especially things that involved other people." Tami was again living life.

My cup runneth over (new and abundant life)

As David ends verse 5 of Psalm 23, he states: "My cup runneth over." Why is his cup overflowing? It is not necessarily because everything is again perfect in his life. This sentence is connected to the sentence before it, separated only by a semicolon. David's life is overflowing with goodness because of the anointing of God that he had spoken of immediately before this.

From a shepherd's point of view, this anointing of oil on the sheep had brought them relief. Now, as summer gives way to autumn, the bugs and flies that had once tormented the sheep begin to disappear as well. Just as the seasons change, so do the seasons of life. As you have walked through this valley, you have experienced, quite possibly, the darkest season of life. Make no mistake, however, it is a season. This season will soon give way to a new season, and many of the things that tormented you during this time will begin to disappear as well.

When David speaks of his "cup" running over, he is obviously speaking of it running over with good things. However, that is not always the case in Scripture. Immediately proceeding Jesus's arrest, we find Him praying at the Garden of Gethsemane. Matthew 26:39b tells us Jesus prayed, "My Father! If it is possible, let this cup of suffering be taken away from me. Yet I want your will to be done, not mine" (NLT). Jesus prayed to "let his cup of suffering be taken away." He knew what was about to happen, and He prayed earnestly that God would spare Him of the torment that lay ahead. However, Jesus also prayed for God's will to be done.

Jesus's prayer was not answered in the way that He had desired it to be. Today we can see why. It was necessary for Jesus to endure his "cup of suffering," so you and I could be released from the bondage of sin. Probably many of you, like me, asked God to spare you the pain of walking through this long, dark valley of divorce. However, God chose instead to walk with you through your suffering. Why? No blanket statement will adequately cover every situation. However, God sees not only this season, but the seasons that lay ahead. Your current sufferings will soon give way to new life, new hopes, new dreams, new goals, and new seasons.

Today, it may seem that your cup of suffering is running over but look up because a new season is at the end of the valley, and like David, you will soon be able to say that your cup runneth over with good things. Again, it doesn't mean that everything in life will be perfect, but it does mean that you will be led into green pastures and beside still waters by a perfect Shepherd that desires the best for you in every season of life.

A change in perspective

As Susan began to emerge from her valley of divorce, she found something on the other side. Even though she was divorced and single and would be for the next decade, Susan found happiness. She discovered joy through teaching, being with her kids, entertaining guests, and strengthening her relationships with friends. She began looking with hope toward the future and lived and loved life.

Don had a similar experience. "I live life today with a whole lot more optimism. Now, I can be more forward thinking." Beth has found new life through "doing things for others and being with the people that I care most about."

Conclusion

"There is a lot to be said in realizing the difference between no hope and tremendous hope for the future," stated Mark. "When I contrast how I feel today compared to then, I was extremely unhappy—very, very unhappy. Contrast that with today, I'm content. I'm happy." Each of these stories display new hope, happiness, contentment, future planning, and new life. Even though all of us walked through the dark valley of divorce, that season of our lives gave way to a new season. The dark days of winter eventually give way to spring, and with it, the birds begin to sing, the grass begins to grow, the trees begin to sprout, and life and beauty emerge out of the previously brown and lifeless ground.

The valley is not without end. The darkness will eventually give way to life. The brokenness of the past will be overshadowed by dreams for the future. Your life will once again be filled with beauty. Look ahead, learn to love, and live your new life, and soon your cup filled with good things will be running over.

Tehillim 23 (Orthodox Jewish Bible): Psalm 23 (Mizmor of Dovid)

Hashem is my Ro'eh (Shepherd); I shall not lack.

He maketh me to lie down in green pastures; He leadeth me beside the mei menuchot (tranquil waters).

He restoreth my nefesh; He guideth me in the paths of tzedek l'ma'an Shmo (righteousness for the sake of His Name).

Yea, though I walk through the Gey Tzalmavet (Valley of the Shadow of Death), I will fear no rah (evil); for Thou art with me; Thy shevet (rod) and Thy staff they comfort me.

Thou preparest a shulchan before me in the presence of mine enemies: Thou anointest my head with shemen (olive oil); my kos runneth over.

Surely tov and chesed shall follow me kol y'mei chaiyyai (all the days of my life): and I will dwell in the Bais Hashem l'orech yamim (for length of days, whole life).

Carrying on with Confidence

There is a light at the end of the tunnel. You may not be able to see it yet, but don't give up. Put one foot in front of the other and monopolize on those friendships you can count on.

—Mark

Even before He made the world, God loved us and chose us in Christ to be holy and without fault in His eyes. God decided in advance to adopt us into His own family by bringing us to Himself through Jesus Christ. This is what He wanted to do, and it gave Him great pleasure.

—Ephesians 1:4–5 NLT

Carrying on with confidence

For the last few months or years, you have been drudging through the darkest valley of divorce. It has dominated your thoughts, emotions, feelings, time, and life. However, time marches on, and with it comes new opportunities, new hopes, new dreams, and new challenges. As you look ahead, you see a blank canvas of your life story waiting to be written.

For some, that blank canvas may look daunting. Do you have what it takes to turn this next chapter of your life into a beautiful picture? The answer must come from within you. Absolutely! You have so many God-given gifts and talents. It is then that you realize there are dreams from years ago that may once again be possible. Maybe you have wanted to start a new business or take a trip, but it just wasn't possible before. As you look at this new landscape ahead, that old dream once again enters into your world of reality. You have wanted to do it, and now, maybe you can.

As you take one final look back, you notice others that are standing at the rim of the dark valley you have just traveled. Your heart breaks for them because you know what they are thinking and the hopelessness they are feeling. However, you also know that the sun will shine again, and hope will eventually spring forth. One of your greatest joys in healing will come when you reach out a hand and help others navigate the valley you have already traversed. You have the tools, you know the downfalls, you have seen the valley from both sides. You can use your experience to minister to others, and you will.

During your journey, your eyes have been opened, your heart has been expanded, and your true friendships have been strengthened. Without even realizing it, you have built a new foundation in your life. This foundation may be even better and stronger than the foundation you had before. You know that life will not always be easy, but it will always be worth living. It's time to get started in building your new life. It's time to plan and dream again. The future is yours for the taking. It's time to carry on with confidence.

Chapter 23

The Return of the King

Let people help you. Rely heavily on God. Don't dwell on the pain. Lean into the pain. Go through every one of the steps. And with each one of those steps comes healing. This too shall pass.

—Susan

Remember, the further away you get from the point of impact, the easier it's going to be. Healing takes time, but healing happens as we worship, as we continue to stay connected to people in community, inside the church, and with friends.

—Don

He is despised and rejected of men; a man of sorrows and acquainted with grief: and we hid as it were our faces from Him; He was despised, and we esteemed Him not. Surely, He hath borne our griefs and carried our sorrows: yet we did esteem Him stricken, smitten of God, and afflicted. But He was wounded for our transgressions, He was bruised for our iniquities: the chastisement of our peace was upon Him; and with His stripes we are healed.

—Isaiah 53:3–5 KJV

King David's story

David had grown up as a young shepherd watching sheep in the hills surrounding Bethlehem. Being a shepherd was a lowly and sometimes lonely job. However, it was during this time of waiting and maturing that David sharpened his skills with a sling, a sword, and a spear. I would imagine that, in David's mind, this perfected art would be used to kill predators as David cared for his sheep. Indeed, this was the case as the Bible tells us of David killing both lions and bears while defending the herd.[46] Only in David's wildest youthful imagination could he have ever envisioned a time when he would use his sling to bring down an evil Philistine giant, but again, it happened.[47]

Little did David know that his years of watching sheep, perfecting his skills, and even killing a giant were preparing him for his greatest challenge of becoming king of Israel. The years of running and hiding from Saul, combined with David's years as a warrior on the battlefield, were developing David's strategic abilities as he learned the land and terrain around Israel. God was preparing David to be king long before David took the throne.

Between David's little town of Bethlehem and the capital city of Israel, Jerusalem, ran the Kidron Valley. It had many foreboding challenges, including steep cliffs, many dark shadows used to hide the robbers waiting for a lonely traveler to come along, and, of course, many caves, tombs, and graves along the way. However, at the end of the valley stood Jerusalem in all its glory. In order for David to make it to the throne though, he first had to journey through the Kidron Valley.

King David's triumphant return

The Bible doesn't give us as much detail about King David's route back to Jerusalem, except it tells us in 2 Samuel 20:2b: "But the men of Judah stayed with their king and escorted him from the

---

[46] 1 Samuel 17:34–36
[47] 1 Samuel 17:39–51

Jordan River to Jerusalem." That is all we need to know. As King David cleared the eastern side of the Mount of Olives, the glorious city of Jerusalem again greeted him. David must have been overcome with emotion as he looked upon this city and his kingdom once again. For four long years, David had been in exile. I'm sure there were many times when he wondered if and when he would ever make it back to the throne. Now, only one thing lay between David and the return to his throne, the Kidron Valley. This valley that led him to Jerusalem as a boy, brought him to the throne as a man, and ushered him out of Jerusalem as a fleeing king now stood before him one more time. This time, however, David was not walking through the valley but rather across the valley.

As a child, this valley had brought fear as David walked the five miles from Bethlehem to Jerusalem. As a fleeing king, this valley had brought sorrow as David felt the rejection of his son Absalom. As a returning and triumphant king, however, this valley brought hope as it marked the final few footsteps leading David out of exile and back to his throne. As he stood on top of the Mount of Olives and looked across that valley and into Jerusalem, David must have thought, if not said, *I'm home.*

(Surely goodness and mercy shall follow me all the days of my life) Hope

If David wrote Psalm 23 as he crossed the "valley of the shadow of death" fleeing from Absalom, maybe he had the foresight to pen the final verse looking ahead to this day when he would return. The return to the throne did not mean that David would never again face obstacles. In fact, even during his return, there was a rebellion against David. This time, though, David chose an aggressive approach.[48] However, David had learned through his exile and through every battle he faced that the Good Shepherd was always going to be there to lead David, and even during the valleys, David was still blessed with many good things from his good and merciful God.

---

[48] 2 Samuel 20

It's your turn

Like young David tending his sheep and perfecting his skills, God has been preparing you for this moment for a long time. Your divorce did not take God by surprise. It may have caught you off guard; but God knew it was coming, and He has been giving you the skills, gifts, family, and friends you needed long before you were ever married. As you come out of the valley and traverse the final mountain, just know that before you lay a new world of opportunities, new challenges, and most of all, new hope.

I'm sure that one other thing crossed David's mind as he stood atop the Mount of Olives. Standing in the valley between him and Jerusalem was the tomb of Absalom. Although Absalom was probably never buried in the tomb he had built for himself, it still stood as a very prevalent monolith in the valley. As David's eyes scanned this very familiar valley, the tomb must have caught his attention as it now had great significance. As long as two years may have transpired since Absalom's death, but this visual trigger must have brought back a flood of emotions and memories to David. Even though he was returning triumphantly, it had come at a cost. Absalom, whom David loved dearly, was dead, and the sting of his death would always be present as his tomb stood out above all the others just outside the eastern wall of Jerusalem.

As you stand atop the mountain looking at what lay ahead, know that it is natural to feel a little pain and sadness deep within. This new beginning also marks the death of what was. With that comes the thoughts of what could have been. Behind you in the valley you are saying goodbye to many graves of broken hopes, shattered dreams, a severed relationship, and so much more. With any loss comes pain, and you have lost and given up so much more than you ever wanted to. The sting of those reminders will always hurt a little, and that's okay.

Jesus and the valley

Jesus knew the Kidron Valley well from his time spent in Jerusalem. After the last supper, Jesus and His disciples walked out the eastern gate of Jerusalem, crossed the Kidron Valley, and made their way to the Mount of Olives to pray.[49] The Garden of Gethsemane sat at the edge of the Kidron Valley at the base of the Mount of Olives. On the way to the garden, Jesus told His disciples, "Tonight, all of you will desert Me."[50] Jesus knew that Judas was about to betray Him, and Jesus knew that Judas would lead a group to the garden to arrest Him. To this point, Jesus had taken the same escape route as David took while fleeing from Absalom. In less than twenty minutes, Jesus could have ascended the Mount of Olives and escaped His captors into the wilderness just like David. However, in the most heroic act of love ever, Jesus instead stopped and prayed while He waited for Judas and the mob to catch up to Him and apprehend Him. Why would Jesus do this? It was because He knew there would come a day when you and I would be in need of a Savior, and He was the only one worthy to be that sacrifice for our sins. Jesus gave up His life, so we could have a more abundant life through Him.

Instead of the Kidron Valley becoming an escape route for Jesus, it became the first leg of His journey from the Garden of Gethsemane. He was arrested, brought back across the valley, led into Jerusalem, taken up Golgotha's hill, and crucified. Jesus walked through the valley because He knew the day would come when we too would walk through the valley, and through His sacrifice, we can now have Him beside us through every dark valley we walk.

One final walk

Jesus would cross the Kidron Valley one final time after His resurrection. This time, Jesus made His way to the top of the Mount of Olives. After giving some final instructions to His followers, Jesus

---

[49] Matthew 26:30
[50] Matthew 26:31

ascended into heaven.[51] However, in Revelation, we find that one day Jesus will again return to earth. Where is His first stop? You guessed it—the Mount of Olives.[52] This mountain that was the beginning point of Jesus's rejection would be the place of a Christian's final redemption.

(I will dwell in the house of the Lord forever) Ultimate redemption

How could David write such an uplifting psalm as he walked through such a dark valley? Maybe it was because David had the foresight to not only see the day when he would return as king but also realize that his current suffering did not compare to the glory that awaited him when he died. David served God, and because of that, David knew that he would someday meet God face-to-face and begin an eternity of happiness and bliss in heaven with Him.

Today, your journey may look bleak, and the valley may look dark and long; but you must know three things. First, like David's four-year exile, your valley will eventually end, and you will once again stand on the mountain as you look with anticipation at the future ahead of you. Secondly, Jesus walked through the valley and has experienced hurt, rejection, shame, loneliness, and emotional exhaustion just like you have. However, Jesus chose to walk through the valley and ultimately die, so He could walk with you as you walk through your valley. Lastly, if you are a follower of Christ, the day will come when you will trade all the pain, hurt, and sorrow of this life for an eternal home in heaven. Your future is bright, and your eternal future is even brighter.

Hold on. Be strong. Take courage. You are not the first one to walk through the valley, and like those who have walked it before, you will come out of the valley to a new chapter filled with many wonderful and beautiful memories waiting to be made. Have confidence. The darkest hour is right before the dawn.

---

[51] Luke 24:50–51; Acts 1:9–12
[52] Zachariah 14:4; Revelation 19:14

Psalm 23 (Common English Bible): A psalm of David

The LORD is my shepherd. I lack nothing.

He lets me rest in grassy meadows; He leads me to restful waters;

He keeps me alive. He guides me in proper paths for the sake of His good name.

Even when I walk through the darkest valley, I fear no danger because You are with me.

Your rod and your staff—they protect me.

You set a table for me right in front of my enemies.

You bathe my head in oil; my cup is so full it spills over!

Yes, goodness and faithful love will pursue me all the days of my life, and I will live in the LORD's house as long as I live.

Healing the Broken

> It comes at a price to know who God is. I don't think you really know Him until you've been broken.
>
> —Alissa

> Even Christians are broken. We are not perfect. We have to work through our junk.
>
> —Don

Now to Him who is able to do exceedingly abundantly above all that we ask or think, according to the power that works in us, to Him be glory in the church by Christ Jesus to all generations, forever and ever. Amen.

—Ephesians 3:20–21 NKJV

Don's story

It seems only fitting, since we began the book with Don's story, to conclude with Don's story. After Don's divorce was finalized, he began putting the pieces of his life back together again. His healing started when Don, at the advice of his counselor, began taking time to worship God, listening to uplifting Christian music, reading the scriptures, and praying, even when he did not feel like it. Don also discovered something else that changed his outlook. It was the Japanese form of art known as Kintsugi. In this art form, the craftsman will break a piece of pottery and then mold it back together using gold. Therefore, the finished product is more valuable than the original.

As Don learned more about Kintsugi, he quickly realized that that was what God was doing in his life. "He is taking our broken pieces and putting them back together again using His grace," stated Don. "It's the idea that God is in the business of redeeming and restoring the brokenness in our lives and making them more valuable."

Your story

As you have traveled through this long and lonely valley of divorce, Satan has undoubtedly tried to tell you that your life is meaningless, that you will never find happiness again, and that you are too broken to be loved by God, the church, or other people. When you look at the shattered pieces that used to be your life as you knew it, believing those lies is not too difficult.

Today, I want you to hear a different story. As you have been despairing over the brokenness that is your life, God has been taking those pieces and crafting them back together into a vessel that is more valuable and usable than ever before. The Bible tells us that God formed us in our mother's womb.[53] Today, God is once again forming you into someone set aside for a special purpose. You are more valuable than ever before because you have gone through the refining process.

After going through this refining process, Alissa can be thankful for her experience. "I wouldn't have picked it, but God gives us what we need sometimes and not always what we want. I would never have thought I needed it, but sitting here today, even with the questions I have and the pain that I feel, I know who He is now."

So where do you go from here? Who do you listen to, and what do you do next? Alissa contemplated these questions, until one day, a pastor friend gave her this advice, "When you are eating chicken, you eat the meat and leave the bones."

---

[53] Jeremiah 1:5

"Not everything everyone says or everything a preacher preaches, not everything that's said that you are listening to is for you," says Alissa. "Don't try to take it all. When people are trying to help you or give you advice, stop. Digest it. Take the meat and throw the bones out." Help is good, advice is good, but you must be true to yourself and what you know is right.

Beth adds, "Forgive yourself. Don't isolate yourself. Talk to God and others and find a purpose." You do still have a purpose in life, although your purpose may have changed along with your situation. Find your new purpose and live life to the fullest.

You may have felt like your life no longer has meaning, however, Susan disagrees. "Life does go on. It does not stop with divorce." Susan continued, "You will find that the sun shines again. You may find love again, but even if you don't, you can find joy in other things. It's not the end of the world. It just seems like it is at the time."

For Mark, this new life has brought a greater happiness than ever before. "When I look at my life today and compare it to what it was," Mark said, "I can't believe how good God has been to me in spite of my failures, in spite of my actions, and in spite of my lack of faith and reliance on Him. I am amazed how God has worked in my life and how merciful and gracious He has been at guiding me into a different phase."

Do you feel broken? Do you feel like a failure? "Don't beat yourself up over past failures," Don advises. Your brokenness today can be used as God's masterpiece tomorrow. Let God put you back together and make you more valuable than ever. "God can take even the most broken life, turn it around, and do something beautiful with it," stated Mark, "and that's what happened to me." God can perform the same healing in your life as He did in Mark's.

Conclusion

Over the course of this book, we have walked this difficult valley of divorce together. We have spoken of rejection, dealt with shame, buried our old hopes and dreams, and even discovered new hope. As we have, my hope is that this book has helped you in beginning your healing process. Make no mistake, however, it is a process. Don't close this book and stop moving forward in your journey. This is not a journey meant to walk alone. "Rely on God and work on letting go," advises Tami. "Also, ask your friends for what you need because your friends don't know. It doesn't hurt to ask." You must learn to open up and be transparent to those you trust the most. They will be most effective in helping you heal when you let them know how they can help.

As David took his final steps through the Kidron Valley, he could choose to look all around him at the graves and caves that cover the final mile, or he could choose to look up and see the eastern gate of Jerusalem just ahead. You see, those graves that cover the hillside are not meant to be a sign of death but rather a sign of hope. Those plots are extremely valuable with some of them being sold for close to one million dollars. Why? Because those buried there believed they will be the first to see Christ when He returns. It is a graveyard built on hope!

You will soon take your final steps in this long valley. There will still be graves surrounding you, marking the hopes, dreams, relationships, and so much more that you gave up during your journey. You can choose to continue to look at each tombstone and mourn the past, or you can choose to look up because just in front of you stands the door to a new life that God has prepared for you. Look up! You have walked through the valley, you are surrounded by new hope, God is piecing your life back together, and a new day is dawning. Take your blank canvas, give God the brush, and He will make something beautiful out of your life.

APPENDIX A

Advice for Someone Contemplating Divorce

This book focuses on those who are traveling through the dark valley of divorce. However, some that read it will undoubtedly be married but contemplating divorce. This is a big decision and should never be taken lightly. Also, the situation leading up to a divorce greatly influences a person's opinion of divorce. For someone in an abusive marriage, a divorce is a reprieve from the abuse. For one who has been rejected by an unfaithful spouse, the divorce is a sad reality. Experience shapes perspective. No cookie-cutter answer will suffice for all situations. With this in mind, I asked those I interviewed to give some advice for someone contemplating divorce. Below are their responses.

Beth

> Make sure that the divorce is unavoidable, but don't sell out and stay too long. If your partner is willing, try to get help, but you can't do it by yourself. I'm not going to sell myself short.

Alissa

> Marriage is a holy and a hard thing. I am a firm believer in it. If you can make it work and not be in harm's way physically, mentally, or emotionally, it's worth it all. If you are in physical

or mental harm, you don't stay. I'm not saying forever. I don't know what God has in store, but you walk out of it; you put up some boundaries and some fences in your life. Marriage is good; it's worth the work. It's worth the suffering. It's worth the hardship. You think the grass is greener on the other side, and you will just get out and find that perfect person. No one is perfect. They are all full of holes, and when you get to the other side of the fence, you're going to be over there; and it won't be green when you are done trampling it. Life is what you make it. Don't stay if it is going to kill you or hurt you in a way that you cannot come back from. But if it's something that counseling and the love of God and hard work can fix, it's worth it. You made a commitment. Honor your vows. They're important. God will honor you if you honor Him.

Tami

Don't! Obviously, if it is a dangerous situation for you, get out. If you are just unhappy with your spouse, don't! It's harder than you can ever imagine. It's harder than you can begin to think. You are going to have regrets, and it's not biblical. If you are just not getting along, figure it out. God wants you to stay together. I firmly believe that people who are in a dangerous situation should get out. If it's just because he is being immature, or he is not giving you what you need, or you are just "not in love with him anymore," get over it. If you have kids, it is a horrible thing to do to them.

Don

If a Christian is faced with a situation where they feel their marriage is hopeless, give God time to work. Counseling is important. Realize at the same time that if the other person is not willing to engage in the process, sometimes divorce is our only option. It's hard to say that, but I think it's true. I can't force anybody to marry me, and I can't force anybody to stay married to me.

Mark

Before you actually pull the trigger and go for a divorce, try and save it. If somebody has even the slimmest possibility of saving the marriage, I think they would be thankful they did down the road; but sometimes it can't be saved. If they are contemplating it, I would advise them to try and get some help. Get some counseling. Try to work on the marriage. If they are in a place where they just don't think that is going to work, you have to draw strength from your friendships and your family, but I would always advise to try and save it.

Susan

Live with no regrets. If both of you are willing to work on it, do it. Seek godly counsel. Pray. Do everything you know to do but then rely on your heart and what you know is right.

Tim

Divorce is a dramatic and traumatic process. It affects not only you but hundreds of people around you. You should never make that decision lightly. However, you should also never make the decision to stay in a marriage where you are getting physically, mentally, or emotionally abused. This abuse can happen to either spouse in a marriage, and abuse can have long-term emotional and mental effects on the victim. In all other cases, seek Christian counseling, seek God, and pray for wisdom. There is no way to give an easy answer that will adequately cover every other situation. Draw close to God and follow where He leads.

Appendix B

Where Are They Now?

As you have read their stories and seen their hearts, you have undoubtedly become connected to those I interviewed. For some, their journey began twenty-five years ago while others only recently walked through the valley of divorce. Knowing their past trials leads to interests about their present lives. While I cannot go into great detail as they wish to live their private lives, here is a little paragraph on each person interviewed and where they are today.

Beth

After losing her second spouse to cancer, Beth again had to walk the dark valley. This time, however, it was the valley of death. These two valleys, divorce and death, are eerily similar. After walking through the valley the second time, Beth looked back and saw a friend just getting ready to walk through the valley due to the death of his wife. Knowing the journey he would walk and wishing to do what she could to help, Beth reached out to her friend. As she began walking beside him, they began growing closer. Their friendship deepened and eventually grew into something more. This was never Beth's intention when she reached out. However, in 2020, Beth and her friend were united in marriage and began a new journey together.

Alissa

Alissa feels that God wants her to use her experience and story to help other ladies who have been abused. Right now, however, Alissa feels that God has placed her in a season of stillness and healing. "This is very hard for me," says Alissa as she is a doer and not a waiter. However, she continues to trust God and believes that He has a perfect plan for her life and for the life of her young daughter.

Tami

Decades after her first divorce, Tami still regrets her decision to walk away from her marriage. Even though she knows God has forgiven her and she has a good relationship with her ex-husband, she still wonders what would have been if she had remained faithful and worked through their marriage issues as a young couple. Tami also lives with emotional scars from trauma she endured during her second marriage. Through it all, Tami continues her career and leans heavily on God for help. Tami has a close relationship with each of her three grown children.

Don

Shortly after his divorce, Don began looking for another companion. Don found that companion who, like him, had suffered the rejection of an unfaithful spouse. Together they walked through the valley as they aided in each other's healing. In 2020, Don and his bride were married. Their ceremony included the Japanese art form of Kintsugi as they gave each of their children a piece of broken pottery that had been molded back together with gold. It will always be a reminder of how God "is in the business of restoring and redeeming the brokenness in our lives and making it more valuable. It was beautiful," stated Don. While Don is hurt that he was never able to celebrate his thirtieth anniversary, he hopes that maybe he will have another chance at thirty years down the road.

Susan and Mark

After being single for ten years, Susan received a rather surprising message on Facebook. It was from Mark. He asked Susan if she would like to go get coffee with him the next time he was in town. That little message ignited a spark that grew. Susan and Mark were married in 2015. Today, they are happily married and so grateful for each other. Susan put it into words when she said, "I always knew there were people who had [great] marriages like this, and now I have it."

Tim

After moving "home" in late 2020, I was asked by my home church to be the associate pastor. I had no intention of staying in the area, but God had other plans. I accepted the job, which came with lodging. In the last year, my ministry has expanded greatly through preaching and writing. I am doing the things I enjoy and growing as a person. God has blessed me with scores of family and friends that love me and have been with me during the most difficult times. I am optimistic about the future and look forward to even better days ahead.

Appendix C

Scriptures and Translations Used

Explanation

At the beginning of each chapter, there is an inspirational scripture verse. Also, at the end of each chapter, written directly to the person going through a divorce, a different translation of Psalm 23 is quoted. (Chapter 9–11 were written to the church. Chapters 12–14 were directed more toward the children of divorce. Psalm 23 translations were not used at the end of these chapters). Below is a list of the chapters, opening scripture verses, and Psalm 23 translations used.

Section 1: The Conflict

> "Since they are no longer two but one, let no one split apart what God had joined together" (Matthew 19:6 NLT).

Chapter 1: Rejection

> "For God has said, 'I will never fail you. I will never abandon you'" (Hebrews 3:5b NLT; *Psalm 23 King James Version*).

Chapter 2: Dark Days

> "Why am I discouraged? Why is my heart so sad? I will put my hope in God! I will praise

him again—my Savior and my God" (Psalm 42:5–6a NLT; *Psalm 23 New Living Translation*).

Chapter 3: Emotional Exhaustion

"But those who trust in the LORD will find new strength. They will soar high on wings like eagles. They will run and not grow weary. They will walk and not faint" (Isaiah 40:31 KJV; *Psalm 23 Good News Translation*).

Chapter 4: Shame

"In You, O LORD, I put my trust; Let me never be put to shame" (Psalm 71:1 NKJV; *Psalm 23 English Standard Version*).

Chapter 5: Triggers

"'For I know the thoughts that I think toward you,' says the LORD, 'thoughts of peace and not of evil, to give you a future and a hope'" (Jeremiah 29:11 KJV; *Psalm 23 World English Bible*).

Section 2: The Cry for Help

"But in my distress, I cried out to the LORD; yes, I cried to my God for help. He heard me from His sanctuary; my cry reached His ears" (2 Samuel 22:7 NLT).

Chapter 6: Loneliness

"What time I am afraid, I will trust in thee" (Psalm 56:3 NLT; *Psalm 23 Complete Jewish Bible*).

Chapter 7: Should I Have Done More?

> "I am leaving you with a gift—peace of mind and heart. And the peace I give is a gift the world cannot give. So don't be troubled or afraid" (John 14:27 NLT; *Psalm 23 Christian Standard Bible*).

Chapter 8: Worse than Death

> "The LORD is close to the brokenhearted; He rescues those whose spirits are crushed" (Psalm 34:18 NLT; *Psalm 23 Amplified Bible*).

Section 3: The Church

> "The LORD is my rock, my fortress, and my savior; my God is my rock, in whom I find protection. He is my shield, the power that saves me, and my place of safety" (Psalm 18:2).

Chapter 9: How Did I Become a Statistic?

> "The LORD is good, a strong refuge when trouble comes. He is close to those who trust in him" (Nahum 1:7 NLT).

Chapter 10: How Will the Church View Me?

> "God blesses those who mourn, for they will be comforted" (Matthew 5:4 NLT).

Chapter 11: Help or Hinder

> "So encourage each other and build each other up, just as you are already doing" (1 Thessalonians 5:11 NLT).

Section 4: The Children of Divorce

> "Ye are of God, little children, and have overcome them: because greater is he that is in you, than he that is in the world" (1 John 4:4 KJV).

Chapter 12: The Children of Divorce

> "A father to the fatherless, a defender of widows, is God in His holy dwelling" (Psalm 68:5 NIV).

Chapter 13: Save the Children

> "But you, God, see the trouble of the afflicted; You consider their grief and take it in hand. The victims commit themselves to You; You are the helper of the fatherless" (Psalm 10:14 NIV).

Chapter 14: Redemption

> "But in my distress, I cried out to the LORD; yes, I prayed to my God for help. He heard me from His sanctuary; my cry to Him reached His ears" (Psalm 18:6 NLT).

Section 5: Cultivating Healing

> "So be strong and courageous! Do not be afraid and do not panic before them. For the Lord your God will personally go ahead of you; He will neither fail you nor abandon you" (Deuteronomy 31:6 NLT).

Chapter 15: Hope

> "Rejoice in our confident hope. Be patient in trouble and keep on praying" (Romans 12:12 NLT; *Psalm 23 New Life Version*).

Chapter 16: The Importance of Healing

> "He led me to a place of safety; He rescued me because He delights in me" (2 Samuel 22:20 NLT; *Psalm 23 The Passion Translation*).

Chapter 17: Help in Healing

> "The LORD also will be a refuge for the oppressed, a refuge in times of trouble" (Psalm 9:9 KJV: *Psalm 23 Expanded Bible*).

Chapter 18: Our Living Hope

> "In peace I will lie down and sleep, for you alone, LORD, make me dwell in safety" (Psalm 4:8 NIV; *Psalm 23 New International Version*).

Section 6: Coming Alive

> "Therefore, if anyone is in Christ, the new creation has come: The old has gone, the new is here" (2 Corinthians 5:17 NLT).

Chapter 19: Loving Yourself

> "Keep me as the apple of your eye; hide me under the shadow of your wings" (Psalm 17:8 NKJV; *Psalm 23 Tree of Life Version*).

Chapter 20: Loving Others

"Bear one another's burdens, and so fulfill the law of Christ" (Psalm 17:8 NKJV; *Psalm 23 Young's Literal Translation*).

Chapter 21: Loving God

"Draw near to God and He will draw near to you. Cleanse your hands, you sinners; and purify your hearts, you double-minded" (James 4:8 NKJV; *Psalm 23 The Voice*).

Chapter 22: Living Life

"To all who mourn in Israel, He will give a crown of beauty for ashes, a joyous blessing instead of mourning, festive praise instead of despair. In their righteousness, they will be like great oaks that the LORD has planted for His own glory" (James 4:8 NLT; *Psalm 23 Orthodox Jewish Bible*).

Section 7: Carrying on with Confidence

"Even before he made the world, God loved us and chose us in Christ to be holy and without fault in his eyes. God decided in advance to adopt us into His own family by bringing us to Himself through Jesus Christ. This is what He wanted to do, and it gave Him great pleasure" (Ephesians 1:4–5 NLT).

Chapter 23: The Return of the King

"He is despised and rejected of men; a man of sorrows and acquainted with grief: and we hid as it were our faces from Him; He was despised, and we esteemed Him not. Surely, He hath borne our griefs, and carried our sorrows: yet we did esteem Him stricken, smitten of God, and afflicted. But He was wounded for our transgressions, He was bruised for our iniquities: the chastisement of our peace was upon Him; and with His stripes we are healed" (Isaiah 53:3–5 KJV; *Psalm 23 Common English Bible*).

Conclusion

"Now to Him who is able to do exceedingly abundantly above all that we ask or think, according to the power that works in us, to Him be glory in the church by Christ Jesus to all generations, forever and ever. Amen" (Ephesians 3:2021 NKJV).

About the Author

Tim Scott has spent most of his adult life working with teens as a teacher, athletics director, basketball coach, house parent, and youth pastor. In addition, Tim served on the "youth council" at Harmony Hill Youth Camp and founded and directed "Compass Ministries," which organized summer short-term mission trips at home and overseas. He currently serves on the Missouri Christian School Athletics Association (MCSAA) committee.

In 2015, Tim published his first book, *A Coach's Heart*, about experiences from his two decades of coaching basketball. *Though I Walk through the Valley* is Tim's second book.

In October of 2020, Tim moved back to his hometown of Lowry City, Missouri, to be closer to his family and close friends. Tim is currently the associate pastor of the Lowry City Church of God (Holiness).

CPSIA information can be obtained
at www.ICGtesting.com
Printed in the USA
BVHW081532251022
650236BV00006B/179